Creating a Culture of Literacy

Creating a Culture of Literacy

Programming Ideas for Elementary School Librarians

Anne E. Ruefle

Libraries Unlimited
An Imprint of ABC-CLIO, LLC

A B C ✷ C L I O

Santa Barbara, California • Denver, Colorado • Oxford, England

Library of Congress Cataloging-in-Publication Data

Ruefle, Anne E.
　　Creating a culture of literacy : programming ideas for elementary school librarians / Anne E. Ruefle.
　　　　p. cm.
　　Includes bibliographical references and index.
　　ISBN 978–1–59158–719–4 (acid-free paper)　　1. Elementary school libraries—Activity programs.　2. Reading promotion.　I. Title.
　　Z675.S3R795　2009
　　027.8'222—dc22　　　2009009958

13　12　11　10　9　1　2　3　4　5

This book is also available on the World Wide Web as an eBook.

Visit www.abc-clio.com for details.

ABC-CLIO, LLC

130 Cremona Drive, P.O. Box 1911

Santa Barbara, California 93116-1911

This book is printed on acid-free paper ∞

Manufactured in the United States of America

To my mother, Kathleen Theresa Noone Ruefle, who, with her wit and creativity and extraordinary sense of family, knows a great deal about raising a whole lot of readers. And to her best friend, Betty Boston, whose love of education inspired at least ten children in ways she couldn't have imagined.

Contents

Acknowledgments

Many, many thanks to the hundreds and hundreds of Saint Mary students and their amazing families, who are such eager participants in so many unusual reading-related activities: attending lunches, spending the night at school, baking cakes, making costumes, cooking pasta, showing up early for breakfast stories, painting cars and boats, going on library field trips, decorating hallways, celebrating birthdays with books, and, of course, sharing their reading experiences with me.

Thank you to my extraordinary coworkers who have allowed me to invade their classrooms, interrupt their schedules, and share dozens of projects with them over the years, with special thanks to Mary Wickham, Bonnie Jones, Joby Easley, Teresa Monds, Amy Stewart, and Roseanne Hanson—you always go above and beyond.

Thank you to Kathy McClernon and Regina Synder, principals with patience for my programs and understanding about my paperwork procrastination.

Thank you to Libraries Unlimited, for providing me the opportunity to share my ideas with a wider audience.

Thank you to my four favorite readers: Emelio, Callie, Eli, and Maria—especially for sharing their mom with hundreds of other kids.

And of course to Rick—my in-house editor, project collaborator, 24/7 tech support, idea man, personal DJ, and constant companion. Thank you.

Introduction

At 12:20 A.M. on the night of July 29, 2007, I was sitting in a camp chair in my school's gymnasium. I had my brand new copy of *Harry Potter and the Deathly Hallows* open on my lap, ready to begin reading the long-awaited final book in this much-beloved series.

I couldn't bring myself to start reading, though. I kept looking around the gymnasium, marveling at what I was witnessing. All around the room were students, ranging in ages from 9 to 19, huddled on top of sleeping bags, lounging on air mattresses, sprawled out on blankets, and hunkered down in chairs. The room was full of lively, energetic, and excited children; it was after midnight, and the room was completely silent. Everyone was reading.

Just 20 minutes before, our large group of students was waiting at the front of a long, long line of Harry Potter fans at a bookstore across the street from our school. We were having a sleepover in our school gym to celebrate the release of the seventh and final Harry Potter book. Current students in grades three through eight who had read the first six books were invited, as well as a dozen or so high school alumni who had been huge fans when they were in grade school.

We had prepaid for our books and positioned ourselves at the front of the line, so when the book was officially released a few minutes after midnight, our school group received several boxes of the Harry Potter book and headed back to our school, walking past a long, long line of waiting customers. A few of the parents and teachers accompanying the group carried the boxes, while the students, thrilled to be prancing down the street at midnight, ran and jumped and cheered and chanted "Harry Potter" at the top of their lungs. No one cared; no one told them to shush.

It took us less than five minutes to get from the bookstore to the school gym, and the students clustered around as the boxes were opened and the books distributed. I had imagined that the students, already excited to be spending the night at school in the middle of summer and exhilarated at the release of the final Harry Potter book, would talk and fuss and run around before settling down with their books. I was wrong. Within minutes of the students receiving their books, the entire room was hushed and every child and every adult chaperone was reading.

It was an extraordinary night. I knew that all across America, folks were waiting in similar lines, hosting various parties and events. I also knew that what was happening in our school gym could not happen if the students were not passionate about books and reading.

This book is about developing that passion in your students. For over 20 years, I have been a teacher-librarian at Saint Mary School in Columbus, Ohio, a preschool–eighth grade school. During this time, I have had the privilege of working with hundreds and hundreds of students. My experiences with those students, and the programs we have used in our school, are the basis for this book. I am hopeful that any person interested in literacy and involved in the educational process—librarian, teacher, reading specialist, parent volunteer, administrator, literacy coach, tutor—will find ideas that can be adapted to the school community, adjusting and changing and improving each idea to fit the situation.

Some students will arrive to school as eager readers; some students will be marginally interested; and others will be reluctant readers, with little to no interest in books. Each type of reader needs to be encouraged and challenged with different kinds of activities and substantial literary programs.

But this book is not just a how-to book about activities and programs. Rather, this book is about promoting an environment that supports and values reading; developing a community where every student is expected to be a reader; creating a culture of literacy where students develop and flourish and grow as literate, thoughtful, and critical readers who want to learn, think, know, discover, and be able to share those ideas.

No one learns to read in isolation. We become readers in a community of other readers. We need to develop school communities that support reading in a multitude of ways, allowing for students to read, reflect, react, and respond to what they are reading. The ideas in this book bring the members of the school community together to share in reading-related activities that contribute to creating a culture of literacy.

Not every activity is for every student or school. Some ideas are easy to plan and implement, while others are more complicated and require significant planning and time commitment. Some ideas are designed for small groups of readers, while other programs involve the entire school. No single idea in this book, used in isolation, will turn a student into a reader. A continual effort, however, to engage students with a wide variety of literary activities can indeed make a difference in developing and encouraging readers.

If planning and coordinating multiple activities seems overwhelming, begin slowly and add just one or two new things a year. A strong culture of literacy is a place where students keep bumping up against reading at every turn. For more than two decades, my goal has been to involve as many students as possible, as often as possible, in reading-related activities. I hope that this book provides a wealth of ideas for creating your own culture of literacy.

Chapter 1

Getting Things Started

Quick and Easy Ideas for One Day, One Hour, or 15 Minute Literacy Activities

The ideas in this chapter are quick and easy—they require little planning; they cost little to no money; they can be used once a year, once a month, or as an ongoing project; and they can be used alone or as part of a larger reading celebration. A librarian, teacher, or parent volunteer can implement these quick and easy ideas. Quick and easy literary activities are designed to generate interest, stir up enthusiasm, and remind students that reading should be celebrated every day.

Reading Drills
Reading Train
Sidewalk Chalk Fun
The Mystery Reader
Book Exchange

READING DRILLS

Most schools are required to practice monthly fire drills; schools might also practice tornado drills, rapid response drills, and severe weather drills. If we believe it is important to teach our children how to respond in an emergency situation, then certainly we need to encourage children to practice "emergency reading" skills! Of course, Reading Drills are done in fun. Students will love a break from the school routine—and they will especially love a surprise break when a Reading Drill is announced.

What Is a Reading Drill?

A Reading Drill operates much like a fire drill: When a Reading Drill is announced, teachers will escort their classes to a predetermined site somewhere on school property—for example, the gym, the hallway, the front lawn, the playground, the art room, or the principal's conference room. Every student (and teacher) should bring a book along to read silently for the duration of the drill; 15 minutes seems to be the optimal amount of time. Students not yet reading independently might take several picture books to browse through. At the end of the drill, everyone returns to the classroom, safe in the reassurance that the school can respond quickly to a call for emergency reading.

How to Plan for a Reading Drill

Prearrange a date and time with all administrators, teachers, and support staff; you might select a Tuesday at 10:15 A.M., for instance. Have each classroom teacher select a location anywhere in the school for the Reading Drill site. It is important to coordinate this aspect of the drill so that more than one class doesn't plan to use the same spot. Teachers may want to plan both an indoor and an outdoor spot for the drill, depending on weather conditions. Teachers should inform students that the school is planning an upcoming Reading Drill, but the teachers should not tell their students the specific date and time beforehand—that would spoil the surprise! As with any drill, the students must be prepared. In this instance, an upcoming Reading Drill provides a good opportunity to ensure that all students have an independent reading book at their desk to read at all times.

How to Implement a Reading Drill

When the day and time arrives, use the school's communication system to make an official announcement. A possible introduction might be, "Reading Drill! Reading Drill! Teachers, please escort your class to your designated reading spot for 15 minutes of uninterrupted pleasure reading!"

Give classrooms a minute or two to gather books and travel to their designated spots. After 15 minutes, use the communication system to announce the end of the drill: "The Reading Drill is now over. You may return to your class. Students, please remember that your reading skills can be used to help with any emergency. We hope you continue to practice your reading skills as often as possible!"

Other Ideas for Reading Drills

Make it a point to include as many support staff as possible. Ask the principal to join a class; invite the secretarial staff, cafeteria workers, and janitorial staff to find a class and join in for the silent reading. If you are trying to create a culture of literacy within your school, every person in the school needs to be included in literary activities. Perhaps you might even persuade some teachers or administrators to wear firefighter hats during the drill.

Giving students time to read is fundamental to developing strong readers; a Reading Drill is a visible statement that the school community considers reading important enough to practice it *together*. As with any periods of sustained silent reading, many students simply need time set aside to read in order to become "involved" with a book. You may notice some students walking back from the drill with their noses still in their books. Active readers may already have this healthy addiction to print, but the reading habit needs to be cultivated in some students. The Reading Drill is a fun way to foster this development.

Another Tip for Reading Drills

Encourage teachers to be creative when selecting a place for their class to read. A fifth grade class may sit in the middle of the gymnasium; a first grade class might like to sit on the stairs leading into the school; a third grade class could simply choose to huddle on the reading carpet in the back of their own classroom.

READING TRAIN

What Is a Reading Train?

A Reading Train is a silent reading time that involves everyone in the school. The catch is that everyone is out in the hallway reading, sitting next to one another, lining the hallways, going up and down the stairs—a continuous "train" of students and teachers all reading at the same time for 10 or 15 minutes.

How to Plan a Reading Train

It's simple to ask everyone to climb aboard a Reading Train. Consult your administrators and teachers, and select a suitable day and time. Unlike a Reading Drill, a Reading Train doesn't need an element of surprise. In fact, you should publicize the day/time for parents and invite them to drop by the school to join the Reading Train. It will help to give some direction to each teacher/classroom ("Fifth grade will sit on the north steps, while the second graders will sit opposite the gymnasium doors"). This is not a complicated activity, but anytime you are asking a hundred (or more) children to move, you should have a plan as to where all those bodies will go.

How to Implement a Reading Train

On the day of the Reading Train, students should already have their books selected. When it's time to begin, students file out of their classrooms, walk to their designated areas, find a spot to sit down, and begin reading. Though it may take a few minutes for students to take their places in the Reading Train and to calm down and open their books, a hush will eventually settle over the school and the Reading Train will begin chugging along.

Other Ideas for a Reading Train

It would be fun to have the principal or another esteemed dignitary in the building begin and end the Reading Train by donning an engineer's hat and blowing a train whistle. Wooden train whistles can be found at many toy stores. If no whistle is available, have someone give a boisterous "All aboard!" to begin the Reading Train. And, as with the Reading Drill, invite the support staff to grab a book and join in.

Another Tip for a Reading Train

Any day will work for a Reading Train, but it can also be used as a quick and easy way to celebrate such literary events as Children's Book Week, International Literacy Day (September 8), or School Library Media Month (April).

Read Across America Day (March 2) is another good day for a Reading Train. This day has become the biggest reading event in the country, and your school should be involved in some way. Why not celebrate Read Across America Day by reading across your school with a Reading Train?

If it seems impossible to have the entire school participate, one classroom, one grade level, or one floor could try a Reading Train on a much smaller scale.

Much like a Reading Drill, a Reading Train underscores the importance of reading and provides precious time for students to read. When a school takes the time to gather every student and teacher and asks these individuals to read, it sends a clear message that reading is important and that it connects everyone in the school. If you are interested in creating a culture of literacy, an annual Reading Train might put you on the right track.

SIDEWALK CHALK FUN

There's something so appealing about sidewalk chalk—maybe it's the bright colors, maybe it's the feel of the chalk gliding over the sidewalk, maybe it's the secret longing in each of us to be a graffiti artist. Whatever the reason, this is an easy, 20-minute activity that students will love.

What Is Sidewalk Chalk Fun?

Sidewalk Chalk Fun is an opportunity for students to announce their favorite books using a rather unusual canvas: a school sidewalk or a parking lot. Give all the children a piece of sidewalk chalk, take them outside, and invite them to write the title of a favorite book on the sidewalks or parking lots around the school. The results don't last long (in a day or two the chalk will fade), but students will ask to repeat this activity over and over throughout the year. The most fun is watching students (and adults) walk around the school grounds, reading all the titles and twisting their necks to read book titles written in three-foot-high letters.

How to Plan Sidewalk Chalk Fun

Check with administrators and site supervisors to locate school property where students can *safely* write on sidewalks or parking lots. Select a week when good weather is predicted—rain and cold just won't work for the type of canvas your students will be using. You might use this activity as an easy way to celebrate an event such as National Library Week, though you do not need an official literary holiday to celebrate reading! Take one group of students outside at a time. A group of 30 students can complete this activity in 15–20 minutes. Each teacher could bring out her own class during a specific week or coordinate with a librarian or parent volunteer to supervise groups of children throughout the week. You might find that doing this activity during recess can be a problem—the additional activity is too distracting. It's better to take a class outside when no one else is about.

How to Implement Sidewalk Chalk Fun

Escort the students to the designated sidewalk area. Distribute one piece of chalk per student, and invite each student to write the title of a favorite book anywhere within the area. Be prepared for the kinds of questions kids will ask:

- Can I write more than one book title?
- How big can I write?

- Can I use more than one piece of chalk?
- Can I write in block letters?
- Can I draw a picture?
- What if I can't spell the title?

However you decide to handle these questions, make sure you give your students time to wander around to read what all the other students have written.

If you are including the youngest students in your school in this activity and they are not able to write on their own, consider how they might participate. You might arrange for parent volunteers to be on hand to help with spelling and writing. Ask an older class to team up with a younger class. Have the older students write the title as it is dictated to them, while the younger students draw a picture from their favorite book.

There are many variations on the theme of sidewalk chalk. Students may wish to draw a picture of their favorite character from a book. Perhaps every title could be accompanied by an illustration from the book. Students could draw significant symbols from a book, or a few students may wish to collaborate on drawing the setting of a shared favorite title. You may want to use sidewalk chalk activities in conjunction with the reading of a class novel or theme. The number of variations is limited to the expanse of your imagination.

Other Ideas for Sidewalk Chalk Fun

Purchase large buckets of thick sidewalk chalk from discount dollar stores or during end-of-summer sales. One bucket will easily be enough chalk for 50–60 students. Bring along a camera—this is a good activity to document; there are lots of fun photo opportunities as students bend and kneel and stretch to write titles in chalk across the parking lot (see Figures 1.1 and 1.2). Save these photographs to be included in your Library scrapbook (see chapter 5).

Another Tip for Sidewalk Chalk Fun

Supervise this activity! Remind students that the title of a book is the *only* thing they should be writing, not professions of love for their favorite music group or television show. Provide some baby wipes or a bucket of water for students to rinse their hands *before* they reenter the building; this is where the sidewalk chalk ends! It is not a good idea to let a group of students enter the building with chalk dust all over their hands unless you also happen to be doing a unit on forensics and fingerprints!

Though this is clearly a fun activity, it is also a good opportunity for students to reflect on their own reading habits. If they are able to select only one title to write on the sidewalk, they'll need to do some careful thinking

Figure 1.1 and 1.2: Students writing favorite titles in sidewalk chalk.

and decision making. Students invariably will discuss possible titles with their friends. Discussing favorite books with other readers is a significant way to create a culture of literacy. As students discuss titles and select their favorites, other students might be encouraged to try to read a title they hadn't considered before. If there is an increase in reading after this event, you can chalk it up to this activity!

THE MYSTERY READER

Get a clue—everybody loves a mystery, and having a Mystery Reader "infiltrate" your school for a day or a week is a clever way to generate lots of interest in reading a good book. It also encourages students to read during moments of free time.

What Is a Mystery Reader?

A Mystery Reader is a faculty or staff member who is designated to be a kind of reading spy; that is, for a certain period of time (a day or two, or perhaps an entire week), the Mystery Reader is on the lookout for students who are reading (see Figure 1.3). Students who are "caught" reading

Figure 1.3: This student was caught reading by the Mystery Reader.

receive some sort of small reward. The students won't know who caught them until the identity of the Mystery Reader is unveiled. Much of the fun of having a Mystery Reader is keeping the person's identity a secret for the duration of the program. At the conclusion of the day or week, the Mystery Reader's name is announced. You'll love hearing all the students claim that they KNEW who the secret person was the whole time.

How to Plan for the Mystery Reader

The first thing to do is to determine when and how long your Mystery Reader will be on the lookout for readers. Though a Mystery Reader could work as a stand-alone activity, it works best when it is connected to a larger event, such as Children's Book Week or National Library Week. Announce at least a week in advance when the Mystery Reader will be on the prowl for readers. A Mystery Reader could certainly hunt for readers just for a day, but a longer period of time, such as a week, provides more opportunity for more students to be caught reading. As always, you want as many students as possible to be involved in your reading programs, because you want students to learn to identify themselves as readers, which is essential to becoming a member of a culture of literacy. You'll need to select a person from the faculty or staff to be the Mystery Reader. It is important to select a person with a lot of visibility with the students. The principal or the vice principal is an obvious choice, but there are other staff members who have contact with most or all of the students: the school nurse, the school secretary, the cafeteria manager, the music teacher, the custodian, the technology coordinator, and so on.

Once word gets out that a Mystery Reader will be around during Children's Book Week, for instance, the students will love to guess who the Reader might be. Better yet, they will make sure to have a book with them everywhere they go in school, just in case the Mystery Reader walks by and happens to see them reading as they walk down the hall to the restroom, or while they are waiting for the bus, or at the beginning of a class period. Knowing they may get caught reading will entice students to have books on hand, and if all goes well, they'll be reading more, too.

Students caught reading will receive a small reward—not when they are caught, of course, because then they'd immediately know the identity of the Mystery Reader. Instead, at a predetermined time, perhaps at the end of the school day, any student caught by the Mystery Reader will receive a reading reward. The reward could be a small treat, a pass for an extra 10 minutes of recess, or a pencil with "Caught by the Mystery Reader" inscribed on it (try a novelty store such as Oriental Trading Company— 24 pencils personalized for about $6). The reward should be accompanied by a note (see Figure 1.4).

How to Implement the Mystery Reader

All that the students need to know is that a Mystery Reader has been selected and will be looking for readers. The teachers, however, know the real story: though the Mystery Reader will indeed be looking for readers, *all the teachers* in the building will be participating by quietly keeping track of

you were
caught
Reading
by the
Mystery
Reader
Congratulations!

you were
caught
Reading
by the
Mystery
Reader
Congratulations!

you were
caught
Reading
by the
Mystery
Reader
Congratulations!

you were
caught
Reading
by the
Mystery
Reader
Congratulations!

Figure 1.4: Mystery Reader notes.

the students in their own classrooms who they see reading. It would be impossible for the Mystery Reader to have access to all the students all over the building all day long—which is why the Mystery Reader needs the help of the classroom teachers and other staff members to be covert "spies." Don't tell the students, though! It would ruin the fun if the students knew that it was just their teachers who caught them reading, rather than some mysterious reading superhero.

The teachers and staff, as well as the official Mystery Reader, will submit the names of all the readers who've been caught to the Mystery Reader activity coordinator (usually the school librarian), who will ensure that students receive the designated reward.

Students could be asked to come to the library at a designated time to receive their reward, or members of the Friends of the Library Club (see chapter 3) could distribute rewards to the students during lunch or at the end of a school day. Public recognition of the students caught reading is an important component of the Mystery Reader program.

Other Ideas for the Mystery Reader

You might consider other ways to highlight the names of students caught reading. Perhaps their names could be announced via the school's communication system at the beginning or end of the school day. You could also create a bulletin board with the words "Caught by the Mystery Reader," and as students are caught reading, their names could be posted. In keeping with the mystery theme, print the names on a paper footprint or on a paper magnifying glass.

Don't limit the Mystery Reader to finding just students. Should the Mystery Reader (or any of the "spies") spot an adult visitor to the building who is reading—a parent, a school board member, a representative from the district office—make sure that person is acknowledged in some way.

If you repeat this activity on an annual basis, make sure a different person is selected each time to assume the identity of the Mystery Reader. It becomes a fun ritual for students to try to guess the identity of the Mystery Reader. Don't be surprised if students try to get inside information from you in advance.

Another Tip for the Mystery Reader

Once the time frame for the Mystery Reader is over, make sure you have an appropriate unveiling of the Mystery Reader. It may be as simple as an announcement over the public address system, or it could be as elaborate as a caped figure stalking into an assembly with a drum roll and flourish.

Staging a dramatic finish to the Mystery Reader activity will solidify the experience for the students and leave them eagerly anticipating the next visit from the Mystery Reader.

To build a community of readers and create a culture of literacy, you must continually reinforce reading at all times. Adding a little mystery and incentive to your literacy programs might help uncover some previously undetected readers lurking in the classrooms.

BOOK EXCHANGE

"Hey—I got an Avi book here; I'll trade you my Avi for your Gary Paulsen."

"You can have my Paulsen for your Avi, but can you also throw in that Aliki book?"

"I'm looking for a *Captain Underpants*; anybody see any Underpants on this table?"

Forget the excitement of the big-city stock exchanges; for real excitement and wealth, try a Book Exchange!

What Is a Book Exchange?

A Book Exchange is a book swap. It is different from a Book Fair or a used book sale in that no money is necessary; the inventory comes from the students themselves. Students simply bring in books from home that they no longer want, and then they have the opportunity to select another book from the Exchange.

A Book Exchange operates as an even exchange: if a student donates three books, then she gets to select three books. A Book Exchange is an easy and effective way for students to get their hands on titles they haven't yet read, while sharing books that have accumulated in their home library. It is a literary version of recycling!

How to Plan a Book Exchange

Select a day for your Book Exchange, and invite students to bring in any books that they would like to swap for other books. Provide at least a week or two to collect books from the students before the actual Exchange. Any day of the week will work for your Exchange, but if you choose a Friday, you will have the entire week beforehand to remind students to bring in their used books.

You will also need to schedule times for the Book Exchange. All of the students participating in the Book Exchange can't possibly come at the same time, so you'll need to consider who comes when.

If your students eat lunch in a large cafeteria, you might try holding a Book Exchange in the cafeteria or in proximity to the lunchroom. Students could "shop" at the Book Exchange during their lunchtime, so as not to disrupt class times.

The best Book Exchanges have lots of books from which to choose, and you can only acquire lots of books if you advertise your Book Exchange well in advance. A marketing blitz, with posters and fliers as well as word-of-mouth advertisements, will generate interest (see Figure 1.5).

In addition to fliers and posters, you might be able to use the school's public address system to make reminder announcements for several days before the Exchange. Teachers can promote the Book Exchange in their classrooms, and students visiting the library should certainly be reminded about the opportunity to trade some of their unused books.

It's important to set some guidelines for the book donations. Be clear that you'll only accept *gently* used books. Let students know that badly damaged or worn books will not be acceptable for the Exchange. Remind students that they would not like to receive books that are tattered or hopelessly out of date. Magazines and comic books get pretty beat up after just one or two readings, so you will have to decide if you want to include these kinds of materials. Make sure students understand that not every book is suitable for a Book Exchange and that adult supervisors have the right to refuse a book that is in poor condition or is not appropriate for a school book swap. Paperback books that students read once but will likely not read again make good contributions. Books purchased through Book Fairs and classroom book-order forms are also apt choices for a Book Exchange.

Make sure students understand when book donations will be accepted. Consider collecting books for two or three weeks prior to the actual Exchange to ensure a large number of books is collected. The school library typically acts as the repository for all the donated books until the day of the Book Exchange.

You might also stipulate that students bring in books suitable for a specific grade level. Fifth graders, for instance, might be asked to bring in books just for fourth or fifth graders and not books for kindergartners. If you don't stipulate this requirement, students might look to clean out their shelves of books they read five years ago, and you could very well end up with 62 books for kindergartners and first graders but nothing suitable for fifth graders. You want to emphasize that this is an *exchange* and that students should concentrate on exchanging within their own reading or grade levels.

Finally, keep track of how many books each student brings in. You might keep a notebook and record each participating student and the number of books donated. As students visit the Book Exchange, check the

All students in third and fourth grade are invited to bring in books for a

Children's Book Week

Book Exchange!

It's a book swap!
It's a terrific way to share your books!
It's a great chance to get some gently used books!
It's a perfect way to clean up the bookshelves in your room!

For each book you bring in, you'll receive a ticket to redeem
at the Book Exchange next Friday.

~Bring in **one** book, get a ticket to redeem for **one** book at the Book Exchange.
~Bring in **two** books, get **two** tickets to redeem at the Book Exchange.
~Bring in **three** books, get **three** tickets . . . get it?!

Members of the
Friends of the Library
will be available to take your
book donations in the library
any morning this week and next.

Remember: no comic books or magazines, please!
We are looking for good, gently used books suitable for other
third and fourth graders.

Figure 1.5: Sample flier for a Book Exchange.

From *Creating a Culture of Literacy: Programming Ideas for Elementary School Librarians* by Anne E. Ruefle. Santa Barbara, CA: Libraries Unlimited. Copyright © 2009.

notebook and inform the student how many books he is allowed to choose. You could also hand out one ticket for each book a student brings in; students then redeem the tickets on the day of the Book Exchange.

How to Implement a Book Exchange

On the day of the Book Exchange, make sure to have enough tables to hold all the donated books. If the Exchange is being held somewhere other than the library, the boxes of books will need to be hauled to where the Exchange is taking place. Take care not to just toss the books onto the tables. Thoughtfully sorting and arranging the books will make for a smoother Book Exchange.

If multiple grades are participating, the books should be divided into reading levels: first and second grade books, third and fourth grade, and so on. If you have enough books and enough space, you could further separate the books into genres such as adventure, science fiction, fantasy, and humor.

Though the Book Exchange generally operates smoothly, it will need some supervision. Parent volunteers are great for this event; they can move and sort the books as well as collect the redeemed tickets or check the notebook for a student's allotted number of selections. Parent volunteers can make sure that classes of visiting students adhere to the schedule, and they can also help an indecisive child make a selection.

If there are any leftover books after a Book Exchange, they could be put into a box with a sign that reads "Free to a good home." Students not able to participate in the Book Exchange may grab a book or two from the freebie box.

Other Ideas for a Book Exchange

All good libraries weed their shelves each year; many of the weeded books are still in worthwhile condition. These soon-to-be-discarded books would be a great addition to an upcoming Book Exchange. Ask teachers, too, for any discards from their classrooms. Sometimes teachers and librarians need to weed their shelves just to make way for newer titles. A Book Exchange is a great way to ensure that the discarded books, still viable and in good condition, will make their way into the hands of a child. It is important, however, to take note of your district's policy for discarding books, as some districts have strict guidelines for the removal and redistribution of discarded materials.

Book Exchanges work well on a schoolwide basis, but Book Exchanges can also be adapted for just a portion of the school. If there are six third grade classrooms, for instance, the Book Exchange could be a special activity just for those six classrooms. Concentrated Book Exchanges are often effective because students feel comfortable bringing in books for their peers and can easily understand the guidelines for bringing a book to trade with someone their own age.

Another Tip for a Book Exchange

A Book Exchange is a perfect activity for your Friends of the Library Club to oversee (see chapter 3). The Friends of the Library could help make posters, hang up fliers, and write and deliver announcements. As the book donations trickle into the library, the Friends of the Library students would love to sort the books according to grade levels. In addition to sorting books, they might assist on the day of the Exchange by unloading boxes, collecting tickets, and neatly displaying the books on the table.

Perhaps the most significant aspect of a successful Book Exchange is that students will necessarily converse about books with other students during the swap. Because no one becomes a reader in isolation, conversation is yet another way to connect with other readers. It can be invigorating to hear the discussions between students as they ask for recommendations and advice from each other; and if two students get into a dispute over a particularly coveted book, it might just be the most enjoyable fight you ever referee!

Chapter 2

Bringing Books to Life

Literacy Activities to Amuse, Entertain, and Inspire Your Readers

In this chapter you'll find literacy activities that are directly connected to books. Though these activities require a bit more planning than the ideas from chapter 1, they are not difficult to orchestrate and can be easily adapted to fit your school's culture. You can use these ideas throughout the year, once a year, as part of a larger reading celebration, or as a stand-alone activity. They allow for collaboration between librarian and teacher, and most of all, they are delightful ways to cajole your students into reading.

Quotes of the Day
Poet-Tree Breaks
100 Days/100 Books
Same Book/Same Time
Breakfast with a Book

QUOTES OF THE DAY

Quick, who said: "Somebody's been eating *my* porridge!"? Too easy for you? OK, try this one: "I'll eat you up!" Did you guess Max, from Maurice Sendak's *Where the Wild Things Are*? Here's one more: "The news reporters found out about the two pigs I had for dinner. They figured a sick guy going to borrow a cup of sugar didn't sound very exciting." It's a line from A. Wolf, in Jon Scieszka's *The True Story of the Three Little Pigs*—and you've just played a simple version of Quotes of the Day.

What Is a "Quotes of the Day" Activity?

Quotes of the Day is a literacy activity that asks students to guess from which book a quotation comes. Trying to guess the correct book can be addictive; students will love this guessing game and will want to play it all the time. Not only is it fun and challenging, but best of all it reinforces the notion that students are readers who share a common language of books.

Quotes of the Day can be incorporated into your school in a variety of ways. It is a wonderful activity to be included as part of a larger reading celebration. If your school participates in celebrations such as Children's Book Week, Teen Read Week, or National Library Week, Quotes of the Day could be an activity used throughout that week.

How to Plan Quotes of the Day

Compile a list of books that are very popular with your students. You'll want to select your quotations from books that are familiar with as many students as possible. This step is crucial. Though you want to challenge the students to recall the source of the quotation, you do not want to select books that are too esoteric or unfamiliar and leave the students completely dumbfounded. A primary goal for this activity is to validate that the students, as readers, have knowledge of books. If a child hears a quotation and recognizes the book from which it came, he will have the immediate sensation that he *knows* the book; knowing books is a sure way of believing that you are a *reader*.

This first step is a good opportunity for collaboration between the librarian and the classroom teachers, because together they can determine which books are the most popular with a particular group of students. A group of second grade teachers can compile a list of books they've shared with their students throughout the year, and the librarian can work with the teachers to discuss the favorite titles that have been introduced in the library.

The number of books on your list will depend on how often you plan to share Quotes of the Day with your students, as well as how many different grades you are working with. If you wish to read one quotation a day for an entire school week, you'll need to select five books. If you are working with multiple grades, however, you'll probably want to compile a separate book list for each grade. First graders and fifth graders would necessarily have different books on their lists.

If you decide, for instance, that three grades will participate in this activity for an entire week, you'll need to select 15 books (one book per day for each grade every day of the week). This is why collaboration between classroom teachers and librarians is essential for a successful "Quotes of the Day" activity; you'll need to work together to come up with appropriate titles for multiple book lists.

After you have compiled your lists, select a passage—anywhere from a sentence or two to an entire paragraph—from each book. You'll want to give careful thought to this selection. You should select a sentence or passage that has some relevance to the story, something that will jar a student's memory so that she thinks, "Oh, yes! I know that book!"

Avoid selecting a sentence or passage that immediately identifies the main character. "Goldilocks knocked on the door, but there was no answer" is just too easy and obvious. The quotation should challenge but not confound or patronize the students.

Sentences describing a scene from nature do not make the best quotations, because they are too vague for a child to pinpoint. "It was a beautiful spring morning when the girl went out for a walk" is nondescript. But a sentence that hints at the main drama in a story would be just right: "Then the girl walked into the living room where she found three chairs, each a different size."

After you have selected your books and chosen your passages, you're *almost* ready to share the quotations with the students. Before you read the quotations to your students, you need to be prepared to receive their answers. A simple solution is to decorate a good-sized jar and label it "Quotes of the Day" (see Figure 2.1). Each classroom that is participating should have its own jar either in the classroom or in the library.

Figure 2.1: A student submits an answer for Quotes of the Day.

Students should be ready for Quotes of the Day with small slips of paper on which to write their guesses. You might have paper slips prepared to make it easier for the students. Have a stack of these slips available to any class that is participating.

THE RILEY SCHOOL'S
QUOTES OF THE DAY
Student name & grade:
Title/Guess:

Make sure students know any parameters for this activity in advance. Information could be distributed to each classroom with a brief memo such as the following:

All guesses for this week's Quotes of the Day must be received by 10:00 A.M. each morning in the school library. The first entry with the *correct* answer selected from the jar will be declared the winner. The name of the student with the winning guess will be announced at lunchtime. Students may come to the library after school to receive their prize.

How to Implement Quotes of the Day

The final step in preparing this activity is to decide when and how you will share the quotations with the students. You might read the quotations to each class as they visit the library during your reading celebration week. Each teacher might receive a printed copy of the quotations to read to her class each day. Perhaps you have access to the school's public address system to read the quotations aloud to the entire school during morning announcements—and consider the way in which reading is validated and highlighted in a school if literary quotations are read each morning during schoolwide announcements!

Once students hear the quotation, they should fill out their slip and put it in the appropriate jar. The first correct answer slip selected from the jar determines the winner for that particular Quote of the Day. The name of the winning student should be announced sometime during the school day. It is important to announce not only the name of the winning child but also the correct title so the rest of the students will know if their guess was correct. Though students might be disappointed that their slip with the correct answer was not selected, they will at least have some satisfaction knowing that their guess was correct. In many ways, this is the purpose of this activity—not to find a few winners but to subtly remind all students that they are part of a community of readers.

THE RILEY SCHOOL'S
QUOTES OF THE DAY
Student name & grade: Luke, grade 3
Title/Guess: *Goldilocks and the Three Bears*

Other Ideas for Quotes of the Day

Because your students will love this activity, you need not limit it to just one week of the year. Consider incorporating Quotes of the Day into the regular school year calendar. You might read Quotes of the Day during lunch on the first Friday of each month. A classroom teacher might like to ask Quotes of the Day every Monday morning to his class.

A very simple version of Quotes of the Day is to read a passage from a book before you begin each weekly story time, and rather than utilize a slip of paper and a guessing jar, just call on students who want to take a guess. This can serve as a quick introductory activity for students as they settle down for a story, and it can be used as a review of stories that you've shared with students in previous weeks.

Another variation is to ask students to prepare Quotes of the Day to share with classmates. Not only will they have fun challenging one another, but also they can develop the skill of reviewing texts and selecting appropriate passages from within that text.

Thankfully, you have an entire library of books from which to choose quotations, so you should never run out of sources for your Quotes of the Day activity, no matter how many different ages of students you are working with.

Another Tip for Quotes of the Day

If you are using Quotes of the Day as a major school activity and you have gone to the trouble of compiling lists, selecting quotations, creating slips, and making guessing jars, you'll certainly need to make sure the winners are rewarded in some way. You'll also need to determine how many winners you will have. Perhaps one winner per grade or class? Three winners in each grade? The size of your school and the number of prizes available will influence your decision here.

You also need to give some thought to how you will reward the winners of the Quotes of the Day. As with the Mystery Reader rewards (see chapter 1), the prizes need not be extravagant. The best prizes are books, of course! If your school hosts a Book Fair that allows you to select free paperbacks as part of an incentive package, keep this activity in mind as you select those free books.

POET-TREE BREAKS

Poetry is an essential form of literature that can be introduced to students in a variety of ways. There are many poems appropriate for children that are short, meaningful, and intended to be read aloud. In addition to the study of poetry in the language arts classroom, you can implement a Poet-Tree Break in your school that will add variety to your school's culture of literacy.

What Is a Poet-Tree Break?

Holding a tree made from cardboard or using an actual tree branch as a prop, drop by a classroom to announce a "Poet-Tree Break." Open the door, wave your "tree," step into the room, read a poem, and then step back out again. It's a kind of poetry hit-and-run.

How to Plan a Poet-Tree Break

Poetry can be shared anytime during the school year, and a Poet-Tree Break is a clever way to bring poetry to the classroom. If you would like to keep the Poet-Tree Breaks as spontaneous as possible, intersperse them at random times during the year. If you would like a more concentrated approach, April, as National Poetry Month, seems a particularly suitable time. You could also concentrate all your school's Poet-Tree Breaks on Poem in Your Pocket Day (sponsored in part by the National Council of Teachers of English [NCTE] and the American Booksellers Association). New York City has been celebrating Poem in Your Pocket Day since 2002, and the first national Poem in Your Pocket Day began in 2008. This annual event's date can be found on www.poets.com.

Select poems that are appropriate for a particular grade or season. Discuss with the teacher beforehand what kinds of activities or lessons the class is currently studying, and find a poem that might be suitable. While building a culture of literacy, poetry can help students find the connection between poetry and history, science, the arts, math, and literature. Don't select a poem that will take longer than a minute or two to read aloud. This is a Poet-Tree Break, not a time for an epic ballad. If ideas run dry, select a humorous poem from Jack Prelutsky or Shel Silverstein—you can't go wrong there.

The students will love the unexpected break from their classroom routine. Let the students think you are dropping by unannounced, *but always coordinate this activity with the classroom teacher first.* The Poet-Tree Break is designed to appear spontaneous to the students, but it is not a good idea to put the classroom teacher on the spot. Provide the classroom teacher with a copy of the poem and any necessary background information about the poet prior to your visit. Finally, as the reader of the poem, make sure that you have practiced reading the poem aloud.

How to Implement a Poet-Tree Break

Once you have scheduled a Poet-Tree Break time with a particular teacher, you just need to arrive on time, open the door, wave your prop, and read the selected poem. You should also announce the name of the poem, the book from which it is taken, and the name of the poet. The first time you drop in on a class, expect the students to be a bit confused and react accordingly. The best reaction from you is to give no reaction at all. Just read and run. Make sure that the students are settled before you read, and make sure that you bring the poem to life in a loud and clear voice. Read the poem slowly enough that the students will be able to comprehend the content of the poem without having the text in front of them. When you are finished reading your poem, repeat the name of the poem, the poet, and the book, and depart as abruptly as you entered. Let the classroom teacher answer all the inevitable questions:

- Who was that?
- What was that about?
- What was she reading?
- Why did she wave that tree branch?

You should act as if it's the most natural thing in the world to walk down the hall with a tree branch in one hand and a poetry book in the other.

Once your students are familiar with Poet-Tree Breaks, expect cheers and other excited responses from the students as soon as they see your Poet-Tree branch waving in the doorway!

Other Ideas for a Poet-Tree Break

Invite the principal to provide a Poet-Tree Break to several classes during the school year. Invite a few older students to read to the younger grades. Even having teachers visit other classrooms to read a short poem is a simple way to reinforce the idea that we are all part of a literate school community. Anyone who is readily familiar to the students in the class could read a Poet-Tree Break. Guest readers will be impressed with the positive responses from the students.

Another Tip for a Poet-Tree Break

Another kind of "celebrity" reader is a student who has graduated from your school. If you ever have a chance to invite any alumni back, ask them to read a poem for a Poet-Tree Break. The alumni will be honored you asked, and the current students will be thrilled that one of the older kids is back to visit. If the reader is unfamiliar to the students, however, you might want to have the teacher introduce the Poet-Tree Break reader so as not to startle the class.

Poetry is all about ideas, emotion, and language. Sneaking it into the classrooms with a surprise Poet-Tree Break is yet another way to reinforce the importance and joy of this often overlooked literary art form.

100 DAYS/100 BOOKS

Celebrating the 100th Day of school is a phenomenon that has been spreading like wildfire across primary schools for the last decade. Students keep count of all the school days from the first day of school. Students bring 100 items to school, wear 100th Day glasses and hats, list 100 things they love to do, and learn 100 words in a different language. Why not add reading to this list by asking a group of students to read 100 books on the 100th Day of school . . . in one hour!

What Is 100 Days/100 Books?

On the 100th Day of school, a group of students will attempt to *collectively* read 100 books in an hour. At a predetermined time, students begin to read, and they will read, read, read, until the 100th book is completed. As students finish a book, they fill out a small, colorful slip of paper with their name and the title of the book, and that slip of paper is used to form a large 100 on a wall of the school (see Figures 2.2 and 2.3). As the minutes tick by, the students will grow more and more excited to see the paper 100 growing, and they will eagerly work to finish their books to ensure that the 100th Day of school is recognized with 100 books!

Name: Morgan
Title: *Tikki Tikki Tembo*
Our 100th Day Celebration!

---

100 Days/100 Books Name: Title:	100 Days/100 Books Name: Title:
100 Days/100 Books Name: Title:	100 Days/100 Books Name: Title:
100 Days/100 Books Name: Title:	100 Days/100 Books Name: Title:
100 Days/100 Books Name: Title:	100 Days/100 Books Name: Title:
100 Days/100 Books Name: Title:	100 Days/100 Books Name: Title:
100 Days/100 Books Name: Title:	100 Days/100 Books Name: Title:
100 Days/100 Books Name: Title:	100 Days/100 Books Name: Title:

Figure 2.2: Sample 100th Day slips for students.

Figure 2.3: Celebrating 100 Days with 100 books.

How to Plan for 100 Days/100 Books

Though reading 100 books in one hour seems like a daunting task, in reality, your readers won't even work up a sweat. The secret to reading 100 books in an hour is to make sure you have the right number of students reading. You need only 30–50 students for this activity. If you have 35 students and each reads three picture books, you'll easily have 100 books in an hour. Fifty students could read two books each—and you'll be sure to reach your goal of 100 books in under an hour. Collaboration between the librarian and the classroom teachers is necessary to determine *which* grades and *how many* students will be involved. Because many 100th Day celebrations, activities, and books seem to be geared toward the youngest grades, this is a great activity for kindergartners, first graders, and second graders.

If your school is small, you might have two second grade classes of 25 students each working together. If your school is large, perhaps every first grade class could be reading at the same time, each class attempting to read 100 books. There are many scenarios for this activity, but however you decide to proceed, one thing is certain: invite parents to participate! Creating a culture of literacy can only happen if families are involved, and this activity is a perfect way to bring parents into the school (see Figure 2.4).

100 days!

Monday, February 4th
marks the 100th day of school
and the
1st grade classes
would like to celebrate the

100th day of school

by reading

100 books

in one hour!

From 1:00 P.M. to 2:00 P.M. each 1st grader
will sit down with a stack of books and

read, read, read

until, collectively, we've read

100 DIFFERENT BOOKS!

And of course we'd love your help.
If you're available, we need parents (or grandparents)
to sit and read with
children who are not quite reading independently.
If you can help, please contact your child's teacher.
(And if you have little ones at home,
feel free to bring them along, too.)

Figure 2.4: Sample invitation to 100th Day celebration.

From *Creating a Culture of Literacy: Programming Ideas for Elementary School Librarians* by Anne E. Ruefle. Santa Barbara, CA: Libraries Unlimited. Copyright © 2009.

Because you will most likely be working with primary students, some of whom are not yet reading independently, a group of parents to read with students is essential. Don't forget to ask the principal and other members of the faculty and staff who might have a few minutes to join the reading during your scheduled hour.

How to Implement 100 Days/100 Books

On the 99th day of school, invite the students who will be participating to come to the library. Each student should select two or three books that she hasn't read before. Picture books are the preferred choice; chapter books or difficult nonfiction books won't work for this project, because they take too long to read. As students check out the books, you can add some anticipation to the event by securing the stack of books with a rubber band and the child's name and telling the child that the books are not to be opened or read until the 100th Day reading challenge begins. Students will be giddy with excitement as they carry their stack of books to their classrooms.

On the 100th Day of school, at the predetermined time, each child should be ready with a stack of books. Students can wait in their classrooms or gather in one large space, such as the gymnasium. Because of the invited guests in attendance, you may want to spread out into the hallway, lobby, or even to the playground on a nice day. There will be much anticipation for the reading to begin, and it might be fun to have the students count down (10, 9, 8, 7, . . .) to the exact second of "Ready . . . Set . . . Read!"

Once the countdown ends and the reading begins, expect a hush to fall over the students as they open their books. One by one the students will finish their books, write their names and book titles on slips of paper, and take the paper to the person assembling the large 100 on the wall. As the large 100 grows, so will the anticipation of the students as the minutes tick away and the books are read. Expect cheers from all the participants as the 100th book is completed and posted.

Other Ideas for 100 Days/100 Books

If you don't have enough adults available to help the younger readers, make arrangements with some of the older students to assist the younger readers. This is a great opportunity for the older students to interact with the younger students, and it is a way for them to be seen as literacy leaders within their school. In addition to having students try to read 100 books in one hour, this activity builds a sense of a community of readers, young and old, all working toward the same reading goal.

Another Tip for 100 Days/100 Books

Make sure you have your camera! There are many great photo opportunities of parents and children reading together during this activity. These photographs could be a wonderful addition to a library photo album or scrapbook (see chapter 5). There is no better illustration of literacy in your school than a picture of a student reading, independently or with a partner (see Figures 2.5 and 2.6).

SAME BOOK/SAME TIME

It is a Thursday morning, 9:30 A.M., and every teacher in the school is opening up a copy of the same book. In each fourth grade room, in the art room, in the music room, in the kindergarten rooms, and in the physical education class, every child in the school is settling down to hear the same book read. The entire school is focused on the same activity at this moment—listening to the same book at the same time.

What Is Same Book/Same Time?

Creating a culture of literacy requires a shared knowledge and experience by all members of the community. What better way to create this culture than by ensuring that every school member knows several books in common with every other person in the school? By acquiring enough copies of a selected title and asking teachers to read the designated text at the same time on the same day, the school community experiences a literacy event that is simple to plan and profound in its enactment.

How to Plan for Same Book/Same Time

Same Book/Same Time necessitates collaboration among the librarian, teachers, administrators, and, quite possibly, the local public library, which can help supply enough copies of the desired texts. This collaboration involves four steps:

1. Selecting a day and time
2. Connecting to the curriculum
3. Choosing a text
4. Securing copies of the book

Choosing the day and time will be the easiest part, whereas selecting the appropriate text will take more work and discussion. Working with the teachers and the administration, choose an optimal day and time for all concerned. Avoid the busiest times of the day, when students are moving

Figures 2.5 and 2.6: Older students reading to younger students on the 100th day of school.

around the most: the very beginning and end of day, lunchtime, recess, and restroom times. Avoid days where field trips are scheduled, because you want to make sure that all students are present in the building.

Once you have selected a day and time, you'll need to move on to the next two steps: connecting to the curriculum and selecting a suitable text. These two steps are necessarily intertwined. You can't select a text until you know the reason *why* you want a text; in other words, you should determine the rationale as to why your school wants to pursue a Same Book/Same Time. Certainly everybody reading the same text is an admirable goal, but the activity will be more effective if this literary activity is firmly grounded in the school's curriculum or objectives. Consider ways in which a Same Book/Same Time will enhance a schoolwide curriculum. If you are asking every teacher—including math, science, art, and music teachers—to read aloud a book that isn't directly connected to their curricula area, you would do well to ensure that the teachers and students understand how the book connects to the entire school.

Is there an important upcoming historical celebration in your city or state? A bicentennial or other milestone? Chances are that there are picture books that celebrate the event, or biographies of the important people involved. Sharing those books can bring historical events to life for young readers and will connect them to the significant events happening in your community.

You may wish to select a book that relates to an annual event. Perhaps the entire school is looking to celebrate an upcoming holiday or season, such as Thanksgiving, Cinco de Mayo, Chinese New Year, a harvest festival, or Groundhog Day. Select a book that will enlarge each child's knowledge of that event. *Thank You, Sarah: The Woman Who Saved Thanksgiving,* by Laurie Halse Anderson, for instance, will give students a fascinating glimpse into an unknown aspect of this national holiday.

Are you hosting an author visit? While schools that host author visits typically immerse their students in preparation for such a visit, a Same Book/Same Time is a good twist on those preparations, since the entire school would have at least one of the author's books in common. (Of course, a Same Book/Same Time will only work if the author has a book of suitable length for sharing.) The visiting authors and illustrators will thank you for having prepared the students, while the students will enjoy the author's visit so much more since they are familiar with the book.

Major events such as the Olympics or the presidential elections present another opportunity for Same Book/Same Times. *Wilma Unlimited,* the inspiring story of Olympic gold medalist Wilma Rudolph, could be shared with readers of any age. An age-appropriate biography of Abraham Lincoln or James Madison could provide an insight to the presidential elections that students might not consider.

If your school is having visitors from another country, sharing folk tales might provide an interesting backdrop for that country. Any study of other countries or cultures would be enhanced with Same Book/Same Time reading selections.

Your school might be concentrating on a specific area of the curriculum for a unit of study. Mathematics? Read *Math Curse,* by Jon Scieszka, as a Same Book/Same Time. Space? Read *One Giant Leap: The Story of Neil Armstrong,* by Don Brown. Animals? Read *What Do You Do with a Tail Like This?* by Steve Jenkins. There are countless situations, events, occasions, milestones, and people that could be celebrated and studied with a Same Book/Same Time.

After your school has chosen an event to highlight and has determined how it connects to the curriculum, you will need to brainstorm possible titles. When making this decision, consider selecting a picture book that can be read in 15–20 minutes. Longer books will be problematic, as it might take several days to complete the text, and you'd lose the essence of Same Book/Same Time. It's important to list several possible titles, because the final step in planning might be the most difficult: securing enough copies of the desired text.

Though your school could purchase enough copies for each class, that would be expensive. One obvious source is the public library. Use the local public library's considerable resources and its endless willingness to help schools to determine whether there are enough copies of the desired title, and make arrangements for those copies to be available at the same time. You may also be able to borrow from other schools in your district through interlibrary loans. If you belong to a professional listserv, you might put a call out to other schools in your area, requesting to borrow a set of books.

How to Implement Same Book/Same Time

Implementing Same Book/Same Time is the easy part. Once the date, time, and text have been selected and the books have been secured, you'll need to get the books to the teachers so that they may become familiar with the book before the actual reading event. Take into account the non-traditional classrooms: music, art, physical education, and the computer lab. Make sure those teachers are aware of the project and provide them with a copy of the book in advance so they can prepare to read the text aloud. Students need to understand that literacy is important in all areas of the curriculum, not just the reading and language arts classes.

This is an activity that should be well advertised; unlike a Poet-Tree Break, Same Book/Same Time should not have an element of surprise.

You want the students to anticipate Same Book/Same Time. Some ways in which to promote an upcoming Same Book/Same Time event include letters to families, fliers in each classroom, and posters created by your Friends of the Library Club (see chapter 3). The more the students are excited about Same Book/Same Time, the more in-depth the discussions and responses to the book.

Other Ideas for Same Book/Same Time

If your school is very large and it proves impossible to acquire 65 copies of the same title, consider having each grade level read the same book at the same time on one day, and then pass the books to the next grade on the next day. By the end of the week, each student in the building will have read the book.

The more time you give teachers to prepare for this activity, the more likely they will engage their students in discussions and related activities. If any class produces a project related to Same Book/Same Time, those projects could be grouped together in a hallway display. Since Same Book/Same Time is all about creating a similar reading experience for the school community, displaying all related student projects together will underscore that community experience.

Another Tip for Same Book/Same Time

In addition to providing a common text for everyone in the school, Same Book/Same Times are a great source for Quotes of the Day!

BREAKFAST WITH A BOOK

In an ideal world, every child is put to bed with a good book. Wouldn't it be great if every child woke up to a good story as well? If breakfast is the most important meal, why not include some literary nutrition as well? With a monthly Breakfast with a Book program, it is possible to offer an early-morning read-aloud to the school community that can wake 'em up quicker than a cup of coffee.

What Is a Breakfast with a Book?

Breakfast with a Book is a program that gathers the student body together for a read-aloud at the very beginning of the school day. If your school offers a breakfast program, consider coordinating a read-aloud during breakfast. You don't want to intrude upon the food service's territory, but it might very well be possible to work out an arrangement where you read a book to the breakfast eaters, as well as any other students who can comfortably fit into the cafeteria.

If your school doesn't offer a breakfast program on a daily basis, perhaps your parent-teacher association could provide a monthly breakfast opportunity for the school. You might be able to provide donuts and juice at a minimal cost, and gather together the school for two early morning treats: breakfast *and* a story!

How to Plan a Breakfast with a Book

You'll need to begin with conversations with both school administrators and the folks who run the food service at your school. If your school serves breakfast and there is room for lots of children in the cafeteria, then you have the right space to attempt a schoolwide breakfast story. Breakfast with a Book likely would not interfere with the school's breakfast program; if anything, it might draw well-deserved attention to an important component of your school's nutritional plan.

Reassure the administrators and food service personnel that you will just need about 10–15 minutes once a month to share a story with students as they eat breakfast. Explain that your goal is to emphasize the power of a story to bring together a community, and that students who are already sitting and eating are a ready-made audience. Showcasing quality literature during breakfast might be unusual, but it will clearly suggest to the school community that your school values reading.

Be prepared with a list of dates you might like to try and a list of potential readers who might be willing to read an early-morning story to a group of students. You could ask to schedule a Breakfast with a Book for the first Wednesday of each month, for instance, or maybe you will schedule a Breakfast with a Book in honor of some other reading event: Dr. Seuss' birthday (March 2), International Literacy Day (September 8), or the day that the Caldecott Medal is to be announced (check the American Library Association [ALA] Web site for the specific date, as it varies from year to year).

Once you get the green light to proceed with Breakfast with a Book, and you've decided when to hold your event, you're ready to select your books and get your morning started.

How to Implement a Breakfast with a Book

There are as many possibilities for Breakfast with a Book productions as there are cereal brands in a grocery store. The simplest version is for someone to read aloud a story to the students as they munch their cereal. Whoever reads the story should be a skilled reader—someone who has a strong voice and is not nervous to read aloud to a crowd of students. It is a good idea to use a microphone to read the story if one is available. Your list of potential readers might include faculty members, students, parents, even members of the community or local celebrities. Keep your ear out for people with a commanding voice; he might be your next reader!

As your Breakfast with a Book program flourishes, you might try expanding your program beyond mere read-alouds. Consider having one person narrate a story as a group of students silently act out the parts of the characters. You might try having multiple narrators for the same story, each person taking on different roles. With significant practice, a group of students could present a Readers Theater. You could use props, costumes, audiovisuals, or music to enhance your stories.

A Breakfast with a Book could be interactive. A reader could ask the students in the audience some trivia questions from a pertinent nonfiction book. Students might be asked to repeat a phrase from a story or sing along during a story that calls for a musical refrain. You could even share riddles and knock-knock jokes from a good joke book (a fun idea for an April Fool's Day Breakfast with a Book). Turn down the lights for a Halloween story. Your format can change from month to month, depending on the story. No matter what format is used, the most important thing is that the students know that the schoolwide gathering taking place is centered around a *book;* what a powerful way to place literacy at the center of the school.

Another important aspect for the success of your Breakfast with a Book is to involve your faculty in several different ways. You want them present at each Breakfast with a Book to help supervise the students. More important, you'll want members of your faculty present simply because you want them to share in creating a culture of literacy. Watching monthly Breakfast with a Book productions can inspire them to select their own books to share and can entice them to involve their class in more book activities. Teachers may even come to you with a suggestion of a good title or offer to read at a future Breakfast with a Book.

Finally, make sure the parents are asked to attend each Breakfast with a Book. Invite parents to listen to a good story before they head off to work; it might be the best part of their workday (see Figure 2.7)! Make sure that parents are invited to bring their younger children who are not yet attending school. Before dismissing the students when a Breakfast with a Book story concludes, publicly thank the parents for taking the time to join the school for story time, and, in a mock-serious voice, commend the adults on their good behavior during the story and invite them back for the *next* Breakfast with a Book.

A library tradition continues . . .

Breakfast with a Book

returns
Wednesday, September 3rd
8:00 A.M.
(in the school gym/cafeteria)

Parents and students:
Please join us for breakfast at school
the first Wednesday of each month.
As you munch your cinnamon roll or cereal,
you'll be treated to a favorite story
(or poem or play or tale) by a guest reader.

We read from 8:00 A.M. to approximately 8:15 A.M.
Reading is always a great way
to start off your day!

Mark your calendar now for the first Wednesday of each month.

Ms. Lorene's 2nd graders will be helping
to present our first breakfast story for the year!

Figure 2.7: Sample announcement for Breakfast with a Book.

From *Creating a Culture of Literacy: Programming Ideas for Elementary School Librarians* by Anne E. Ruefle. Santa Barbara, CA: Libraries Unlimited. Copyright © 2009.

Other Ideas for a Breakfast with a Book

Though this section is called "Breakfast with a Book," it could just as easily be called "Lunchtime/Storytime" or possibly "Friday Reading Fest." Every school community can adapt the "Breakfast with a Book" idea to suit its special situation. Why not try reading a story during a lunch period? Students might very well sit still and actually finish their sandwiches and milk if they are tuned into a good story. Perhaps the school might gather together on a Friday afternoon once a month to hear a story read aloud right before the dismissal bell.

Another idea is to present a story to the adults who help run your school. Are there monthly parent-teacher association meetings? Offer to present a story with a group of students at the beginning of the meeting. Is there a local school board that meets in your school building? Bring a story to life for those folks. Not only can a story presentation allow the parent-teacher association or school board to see the children fully engaged in a literary activity, but it also raises the visibility of the library in the eyes of some very important stakeholders.

Another Tip for a Breakfast with a Book

The secret to holding regularly scheduled, dynamic read-alouds with the entire school isn't finding the best venue or deciding the most opportune time or day, though certainly both of these are important considerations. The secret to holding successful read-alouds is selecting the right *books.* Many distinguished books don't always translate into great read-alouds. Books that are dependent on their pictures to tell significant parts of the story will not work for a Breakfast with a Book production. Traditional folk tales are one of the best sources; their origins as oral stories lend themselves to being read aloud to large groups. In our highly visual society, a Breakfast with a Book program that emphasizes *listening* can be a refreshing alternative to all the visual images that bombard us. A strong Breakfast with a Book program can wake up the dormant reader in even the most resistant of students.

Chapter 3

Connecting with Kids

Create a Community of Readers—Readers Who Share Their Love of Reading with One Another—with a Variety of Literacy Programs

No one learns to read in isolation. Students develop as readers by connecting with other readers. This chapter offers concrete suggestions for ways to create a culture of active readers by providing opportunities for students to connect, converse, and challenge one another.

Friends of the Library Club
Book Clubs
Literary Lunches
Caldecott Book Club

FRIENDS OF THE LIBRARY CLUB

Most public libraries are supported by Friends of the Library—extraordinary organizations that offer financial support, volunteer hours, and innovative ideas that keep libraries strong and vigorous. Why not arrange for a student version of a Friends of the Library organization?

What Is a Friends of the Library Club?

The thrust of a student Friends of the Library is a library club involving students who are willing to contribute their time and talents to the library.

These are the students who probably are already helping you hang up bulletin boards, staple together papers, run small errands—all of the things students can be so eager to do. A Friends of the Library Club organizes the student activities, providing a way for the students to become more committed and establishing a deeper connection to their school library.

How to Plan a Friends of the Library Club

The first thing you should do is determine what kinds of activities your Friends of the Library Club will do and determine how students can contribute to the library. Advertise what the group is about and let students choose whether to join (see Figure 3.1).

Consider how many students you will need to fill those responsibilities. Be sure to keep the Friends of the Library to a manageable number. Unless you set some guidelines, 75 students might sign up, and you would be scrambling to oversee a very large group. How would they all meet together? Could you have them all come to the library at the same time to help with projects? You might want to invite students from a specific grade level. Make it a special club just for fifth graders, for instance, and let other students know that they'll have a chance to be a Friend of the Library when they are in the fifth grade.

If you need to limit your group to a small number of students and there is a strong possibility that 100 students might be interested, consider having a Friends of the Library application for students to fill out. Students might have to have a letter of recommendation from a teacher in the building, or write a brief essay explaining why they would like to be part of a Friends of the Library group. Using these applications, select the students you feel will make the best group of helpers.

If you open up the application process to everyone and 75 genuinely interested students still show up, and you are comfortable overseeing a large number, then those students can be scheduled to help on a rotating basis. Expect that, initially, a large number of students will be interested, but because of conflicting schedules, various activities, and the sometimes fickle nature of young people, some students will lose interest. Rather than stressing out over students leaving the group, know that the students who stay throughout the school year will be dedicated friends and committed to helping the library.

How to Implement a Friends of the Library Club

Once you have gathered together your group, you need to make sure they are involved on a regular basis. You might ask students to come to the library every Tuesday and Thursday during recess. Does your school

All 5th graders are invited to become a
Friend of the Library

We'll meet Tuesdays and Thursday at recess.

The Friends of the Library Club will help:

-decorate for holidays
-organize the annual Book Exchange
-create bulletin boards
-keep the shelves straight
-prepare for library events
-staple, cut, glue, paint, and color stuff
-and *much, much more*!

If you are interested in joining our Friends of the Library Club, please have a parent or guardian sign the bottom part of this letter and return to the library by September 17.

- -

My child _____ has my permission to join the Friends of the Library.

I understand that the club will meet twice a week during recess.
Parent signature:

Figure 3.1: Sample invitation for a Friends of the Library Club.

From *Creating a Culture of Literacy: Programming Ideas for Elementary School Librarians* by Anne E. Ruefle. Santa Barbara, CA: Libraries Unlimited. Copyright © 2009.

provide study halls for students? Friends of the Library could receive a pass to help in the library during a scheduled study hall. Maybe you'll meet once a month after school. Ask the students for their input; they will be eager for a chance to participate and make suggestions. The main thing is to make sure the students are engaged on a regular basis. Nothing deflates eagerness faster than boredom. Keep the students busy! There are any number of things a student Friends group could do:

- Decorate for holidays
- Learn to shelve books
- Clean and straighten shelves (you might assign each Friend of the Library several shelves to be her very own to straighten and organize each week)
- Prepare for reading celebrations such as Turn Off TV Week or National Library Week
- Hang up posters and signs
- Help with projects such as Book Exchanges (see chapter 1)
- Help check in or check out books
- Create bulletin boards
- Pull books for teacher collections
- Arrange book displays
- Prepare letters for the Birthday Book program (see chapter 5)
- Staple, fold, color, trace, cut out, copy, paint . . .

With proper introduction and experience, many students can become so comfortable helping out that they will need little assistance to complete their work or assigned tasks. With lots of initial instruction and continual dialogue, a student Friends of the Library Club can be instrumental in helping with all the projects you oversee as you work to create a culture of literacy in the school.

Other Ideas for a Friends of the Library Club

Create special nametags for the students to wear while they are helping in the library. It will provide a sense of authority and allow other library users to see that the students are acting in an official capacity. Keep those nametags in the library so you are not continually replacing lost badges.

Another Tip for a Friends of the Library Club

A successful Friends of the Library organization quickly becomes an instrumental part of your library, and you should show your appreciation to this group in some way. If your school holds an awards assembly at the end of the year, publicly acknowledge your Friends of the Library at that time. If you send out a library newsletter (see chapter 5), include information about who is in the group and the tasks the group performs. Perhaps a privilege of being a Friend of the Library is to receive a Birthday Book for half the cost of the regular donation price. Of course, at the end of the school year, you'll need to throw a party for the club—just to show you couldn't get by without a little help from your Friends.

BOOK CLUBS

Of all the activities that can promote a culture of literacy, a Book Club might have the most direct impact on students. Inviting students to become part of a group of readers—readers who choose to read and to come together to discuss what they are reading—is a significant way to further develop a culture of literacy. No one learns to read in isolation; students need time *together* to talk about what they are reading, to share their ideas, to argue about books, and to respond to what they are reading with their peers. A Book Club allows for that kind of intense literary interaction.

What Is a Book Club?

A Book Club is an organized group of readers who gather together on a regular basis throughout the course of the school year to discuss selected books (see Figure 3.2). A student Book Club typically has at least one adult leader, though the students select, read, and discuss the books.

How to Plan a Book Club

Book Clubs are popping up all over the country; there's no reason why your school shouldn't have a Book Club—or two—of its own. There are plenty of questions to consider while planning a Book Club at your school, and the answers to those questions are determined according to the various circumstances of individual schools. Sometimes school librarians hesitate to begin Book Clubs because they feel uncertain as to the "correct" way to run a school-related Book Club. The most important thing to understand is this: *there is no one way to host a Book Club.* If you are gathering together students who are talking about books, then your Book Club is successful.

Though there are no set rules for organizing and moderating a Book Club, there is a list of questions for you to consider that can help you begin a Book Club in your school.

What group do you want to target? Will it be open to the entire school population? Do you want to make it a special program just for middle grade students? Perhaps you want to invite just fourth graders? It's probably

Oprah's doing it . . .
Entire cities are doing it . . .
Why not us?

Join one of the 4th grade Book Clubs!

The girls will meet for the first time on September 12
The boys will meet for the first time on September 13
in the library
at lunchtime

During this meeting, we will talk about what BOOKS
we will read this year.
We will also talk about the two MOVIES we plan on
attending
(after we read the book, of course!)

You bring your lunch and
I'll provide drinks and dessert
(and a door prize or two).

*All you need to join the Book Club is a willingness to try to
read the selected book each month.*

Please join us!

Figure 3.2: Sample Book Club invitation.

best to limit your Book Club to a certain grade or level so that similar reading interests and abilities can be targeted.

What size group do you want? What size group can you accommodate? You need to consider not only space limitations but also the number of students you think will allow for the best literary conversations. You can host a successful Book Club with just three or four interested students, but you need to be prepared in the event that many students are interested. Should 39 students sign up, can that many students engage in a meaningful discussion about a book? Are you willing to host multiple book groups if there is an interest? You might consider dividing a large Book Club into two sections, one for boys and one for girls. Book Clubs separated by genders are increasing in popularity. One benefit of having both a Boys Book Club and a Girls Book Club is that often the book selections for the group are easier to decide if the Book Club is a single-gender club.

When will you meet? During lunch? During recess? Study hall? After school? In the evening? Your schedule, or the schedule of the adult moderator, will probably dictate this decision. Find a time that will accommodate as many students as possible. If few students have access to alternative transportation in the afternoons, then an after-school Book Club might not be the best option. Planning your meetings to avoid scheduling conflicts will allow the greatest number of interested students to attend. The fewer roadblocks, the more likely the students will join.

How often will you meet? Do you want to meet once a month? Once a week? Twice a month? The answer is dependent on your schedule. Most adult Book Clubs typically meet once a month. Because you are working with students, you may want to meet more frequently to ensure that students keep up with the reading. Once you decide on a schedule, you would do well to remind Book Club members of upcoming meetings. Though dedicated readers they might be, busy students they certainly are, and they will need reminders throughout the year. Remember to check with the school administrators to make sure your Book Club dates get put on the calendar and do not conflict with other scheduled school activities.

How long do meetings last? While Book Club meetings for adults can last for hours as the grown-ups talk on and on, the attention spans and ages of students suggest a school Book Club will need considerably less time. A typical school Book Club meeting comfortably lasts only 30–40 minutes. Factor into the length of meeting time the reality of student behavior: students will come to the meeting spot, find a seat, change their seat depending on where their friends are sitting, jostle their belongings for several minutes, and gobble up any snacks and food you might offer. Once each student is settled, you might end up with 20 minutes for actual book discussion. Understanding student behavior will help you adjust your expectations for the time frame you have for real discussion. What matters most is that students have been reading and are gathering to discuss their readings. Make the most out of whatever time allotment you have.

Where will you meet? In a classroom? A multipurpose room? In the library? Will the space allow food and drink? If a Book Club group meets in the library, will it disturb other students or classes? Your space must allow for conversation, intense discussion, and probably a dose of laughter. Though no one likes to see a school library closed during the school day, a Book Club meeting seems like a legitimate reason to close the library to other patrons for an hour or so once a month if necessary. Whatever arrangements you make for space, don't forget all the details of behind-the-scenes work: setting up the room, cleaning up, emptying trash, and returning the room to its original setting. Students will be happy to assist if you ask them to pitch in.

What will you read? This is easily the most fun (because you will never ever run out of choices) and the most problematic (because you will never ever run out of choices). Who decides what books to read? Is it exclusively the domain of the adult leader, or do the students have a voice? One good solution is to have students suggest many book titles at your very first meeting, and then, relying on your expertise, narrow down the choices to a manageable few. You will have insights into what books would be suitable for a group of students to read and discuss. Students are often passionate when pleading for a book to be selected. Listen to their suggestions carefully, but also reserve your veto power. Consider such factors as length, subject material, and availability.

If your group is composed of avid readers who devour anything in print, length need not be a limitation. Let them pursue as many long, challenging books as they can handle. More than likely, though, your group will comprise students with a variety of reading abilities and tastes, so you will want to guide your students to books that appeal to many kinds of readers. The quickest way to kill interest in the Book Club is to select books that are formidable for a majority of the readers. There are literally thousands of choices; your group will certainly settle on several titles of varying lengths to suit everybody.

A Book Club, even if taken very seriously by the members, is not an academic class. Therefore, allow your students freedom to choose books they might not read in their language arts classrooms. You might try a graphic novel, a nonfiction title, or a short and sweet romance novel. Look at award-winning books. All 50 states have some sort of award to honor children's books; consider reading a title from your state's list of winners. If you have organized your Book Clubs by gender, the book lists for each group might be very different—and you might have an easier time deciding on book selections. You might suggest a title that appeals to *both* groups for the last Book Club meeting of the year, and host a joint gathering for both the Boys Book Club and the Girls Book Club. Individual books might have different appeal for your various members, but books can serve as a unifying force as well.

Pay particular attention to the suitability of a reading selection. You want lively discussions, certainly, but you might not want to cause controversy by selecting books that might upset or offend group members. If your Book Club is determined to pursue a book that is edgy or contains violence or difficult subject material, you might inform parents of the reading choice and let the families decide if their child will participate that month. On the other hand, you needn't avoid all books that will generate debate or dissenting voices; your students will love a vigorous discussion, and they will benefit from an engaging discussion of a book.

Realistically, not every title will appeal to every reader, but during the course of a school year, every student in your Book Club will discover a title or two that is mesmerizing—and that's what a Book Club is all about.

How do you acquire copies of selected books? A particularly challenging practical issue of a Book Club is ensuring that every member of your Book Club has access to the same title at the same time. Even if your school library has seven copies of Louis Sachar's *Holes*, for instance, what if you have 15 students in your club? Once again, turn to your public library for assistance. You can choose a book depending on whether the public library has enough copies in its collection. Collaborate with classroom teachers to see if there are titles among their class sets of books that your Book Club could possibly read. You might request titles from other schools in your district. Many school libraries host Book Clubs, and they all have the same dilemma of acquiring enough copies of a book; you could develop a cooperative system for sharing books. Plan your titles a few months in advance to give both you and the students enough time to get your hands on the books. And it's always worth asking if there are funds for purchasing additional copies of a book that is sure to be read by Book Clubs for years to come.

Consider, too, students in your group with special learning needs. You might need to ensure that the selected titles are available as an audio book so that every student who wishes to be in the Book Club can participate. If no audio book is available for a given title, and you have students who are willing to eat their lunch in the library for a week or two, you could arrange to have the book read aloud during lunch. Such an undertaking would be most time consuming, but a commitment to help struggling readers or students with learning disabilities is vital to making sure that every student is part of your culture of reading. You might enlist the aid of other readers (parent volunteers, older students, teacher's aids) to take turns reading the book over a series of days. Even students without any special learning needs often show up to hear a book read aloud, simply for the pleasure of it.

Last but not least, what about food? Food and books go together like pen and paper. If you are hosting a Book Club, you've got to have snacks, though you are not obligated to provide an entire meal. If you are meeting during lunch, require students to bring their own lunches, and you can offer a light snack. Nothing elaborate is necessary; chips and salsa, brownies, cookies, pretzels, or watermelon slices will do. Keep it simple, keep it inexpensive, and keep napkins on hand.

How to Implement a Book Club

You have answered every question regarding the where, when, what, how many, and how often for your Book Club. You've had your initial meeting with students and together you've generated a long list of possible titles, narrowed that list to a manageable number, and selected the first book for students to read. The students are scheduled to be in your library at 3:00 this afternoon for your first-ever book discussion. So, what do you do?

If the students are unfamiliar with one another, introductions should be made. After introductions are made and snacks are passed around, it helps to establish some ground rules. Your students could contribute suggestions for your Book Club rules. Possible ideas for ground rules might include, but are not limited to, the following:

- One person speaks at a time
- Respect opinions of others
- It is acceptable to dislike a book and share that opinion
- Everybody should try to contribute at least one comment each meeting
- It is OK to attend a Book Club meeting even if you haven't finished the book, with the understanding that the end of the book may be discussed
- No rude noises
- Help with cleanup; recycle when possible

Once you have settled on ground rules, it's time to dig into the book. You could easily begin with a basic question: "OK, let's see a show of hands. Who loved this book?" This kind of simple question only takes you so far, but it helps get the students to look around the room and get a sense of the general feeling toward the book. Be prepared, though, with several questions to move the discussion forward. If you have trouble generating possible questions for a book, go online and do a search for the selected book. Many popular books have teacher's guides available that will provide all sorts of discussion questions. Following are other common questions you might ask to nudge the readers when a discussion wanes:

- Why this title for the book?
- Which character would you like to be your classmate?
- Is this an honest depiction of teenagers (or adults or 11-year-olds or cats)?
- How is the setting important to the story? Would this story work in your neighborhood?
- Were there any parts of the book that you think the author should have left out?
- Have you read any other books similar to this one?

After you've been meeting with your students for a while, consider asking students to prepare their own questions. You might assign two students per book to prepare questions, but you don't want to make the Book Club too much like a homework assignment. Part of the pleasure and freedom of a Book Club is that it is *not* required; students choose to join, so don't attach too many requirements.

You'll learn that each Book Club will have distinct personalities; there will be passionate readers and marginal readers. Some students will love everything; other students will find fault with every text. However those reading personalities emerge, allow the students to do the majority of the talking. As moderator, you should keep a discussion going, but the discussion needs to belong to the students. You may have to spark the discussion with a few questions, intervene when necessary, or clean up spills, but let the kids talk. That's a description of a successful Book Club.

Other Ideas for a Book Club

While you are deciding on book choices, keep your sights on upcoming movies. If a suitable movie based on a children's book will premiere during the school year, consider including the book as one of your reading selections and make arrangements to take the students on a movie field trip (see chapter 4). It is essential that students read the book prior to seeing the movie. After the movie, make arrangements to compare and contrast the film to the book. Be prepared for some vigorous discussion! Critical viewing, as well as critical reading, is an important component of literacy, and students typically respond to a book/movie comparison with much enthusiasm.

Though you will most likely be the moderator for your school's Book Club, invite other adults in the building to join you. Publish a list of the upcoming books on your school Web site or in the faculty lounge, and ask teachers to read a book and drop in for a discussion. Invite school administrators to select at least one book during the year to read and discuss with the students. If the chance to exchange literary views with a roomful of earnest readers isn't enough to get them to attend, tell the adults that dessert will be available. That should do the trick.

Another Tip for a Book Club

An easy way to remind students about upcoming Book Club meetings is to make bookmarks with pertinent information (see Figure 3.3). If you are well prepared, you might list on the back of the bookmark some questions for students to consider. All you really need, however, is to provide the title and the date of the meeting. The bookmarks can be as simple or elaborate as you have time or inclination. You can print them on a color or black-and-white copier and attach to some colorful tag stock or construction paper. Once you have a bookmark template made in your word processing files, you need only change the title and date each month. It's easy and effective, and the students will collect them like trading cards.

LITERARY LUNCHES

While Book Clubs are a great way to create a circle of dedicated readers, a Literary Lunch invites a wider group of students to discuss a particularly popular series, topic, or author. Literary Lunches, as single events, can be used in addition to or as an alternative to Book Clubs. A Literary Lunch engages more students in reading activities, can be scheduled anytime during the school year, and is less structured than a Book Club.

What Is a Literary Lunch?

Much like a Book Club, a Literary Lunch is a gathering of readers for a book discussion. Students gather in the library (or other suitable meeting area), bring their lunches, and talk about books. Unlike a Book Club, the Literary Lunch is a *one-time-only* gathering, and the students *aren't all reading the same title*. A Literary Lunch is centered on an author, a subject, or a series, and every person in attendance can read something from within that framework. In this way, readers do not have to worry about finding a copy of the same book, because there is a wider choice of books from which to choose.

You decide when and how often you would like to host a Literary Lunch, and you select the focus of the Lunch. You might host one a month, or you might host two or three a year, inviting a different group each time and

Sample Book Club bookmarks

Figure 3.3: Sample Book Club bookmarks.

From *Creating a Culture of Literacy: Programming Ideas for Elementary School Librarians* by Anne E. Ruefle. Santa Barbara, CA: Libraries Unlimited. Copyright © 2009.

varying the focus of the Literary Lunch. Your schedule and circumstances will dictate the frequency and focus of the Literary Lunches. Students who are hesitant to commit to a year-round Book Club might try a Literary Lunch to see what a reading gathering is all about; eager readers not yet in a Book Club will relish the chance to gather with other readers while waiting for a chance to participate in your Book Club.

How to Plan a Literary Lunch

The first thing you should do is determine what group you wish to invite for a particular lunch. Perhaps you have a thriving sixth grade Book Club and fifth graders are clamoring for a reading club of their own, but you just can't manage hosting another Book Club for them. Instead, organize a Literary Lunch for the eager fifth graders. Select a day and let the fifth graders know there is an upcoming Literary Lunch that is just for them (see Figure 3.4). Now you must select a focus for the group. All you have to do is look around your library for possibilities. Maybe there is a book series that has been gaining in popularity. Capitalize on that popularity and announce that any fifth grader who reads a book in the series may come to the next Literary Lunch.

Give students enough time to read the book; a month's notice is usually adequate. Advertise the Literary Lunch on your school Web site and on fliers posted in and around the fifth grade classrooms. Ask students who are already fans of the series to encourage their classmates to read a book in the series; students make the best ambassadors for books they love.

Determine how many students you can host. If you want to have a discussion or interaction of any kind at the Literary Lunch, you probably have to limit your lunch to a manageable number. You might consider accepting the first 25 students who finish the book, and making attendance at the Literary Lunch subject to whether the student has read the book. A "screening" process of some sort will help prevent an unmanageable number of students from showing up for your Literary Lunch. You do not need an extensive examination process. If your school participates in Accelerated Reader or Reading Counts, those computerized tests can help determine whether a student has read the book. You might also just ask the students several questions of your own to assess whether they have read the book.

If your Literary Lunch goes well, try to host several during the course of a year, varying the topic and inviting different classes or grades. Some possible topics around which to host a Literary Lunch are discussed below.

Focus on an author (see chapter 7). Author studies are hallmarks of strong literary programs; both classroom teachers and librarians often

5th grade Literary Lunch

featuring the books of author

Betty Ren Wright

Friday, January 27

12:00 in the library

In order to attend the 5th grade Literary Lunch,
you need to read at least one book by
Betty Ren Wright

You may pack your lunch ~or~ order from the school cafeteria.
We'll provide drinks, desserts, a door prize or two,
AND some great literary conversation.

Join us!

Some titles by Betty Ren Wright:

The Dollhouse Murders
A Ghost in the House
The Ghosts of Mercy Manner
Christina's Ghost
A Ghost in the Family

Figure 3.4: Sample invitation to a Literary Lunch.

From *Creating a Culture of Literacy: Programming Ideas for Elementary School Librarians* by Anne E. Ruefle. Santa Barbara, CA: Libraries Unlimited. Copyright © 2009.

introduce authors to their students. Centering a Literary Lunch around an author will reinforce the author study and is perhaps the standard reason to host a Literary Lunch. Every student who attends simply has to read a book by the selected author.

Connect with an individual classroom. Perhaps the sixth grade social studies teachers have their students wildly enthusiastic about the Middle Ages. Host a Medieval Literary Lunch, asking students to read a fiction book with the Middle Ages as the setting. Gather together a suitable collection of books about the Middle Ages from your library. Direct your students to titles such as *The Midwife's Apprentice* or *Catherine, Called Birdy,* by Karen Cushman; *The Door in the Wall,* by Marguerite deAngeli; or *The Sword in the Tree,* by Clyde R. Bulla. Invite the social studies teachers to join you for the lunch, and ask the teachers to encourage their students to attend. For additional fun, make paper crowns for the students to wear, and serve hot cross buns as a dessert. As the students enter the library for the Literary Lunch, play chamber music in the background. This kind of Literary Lunch—connecting to an individual classroom or a specific subject—can be played out in hundreds of ways, as long as you can locate books related to the subject, for example, the Underground Railroad, the American West, animals, the Revolutionary War, family stories, outer space, or baseball.

Highlight a popular series. Never miss an opportunity to capitalize on a series that is gaining in popularity. Students who already love the series will be thrilled that you are recognizing their interests, while other students can be steered toward this series. Ensure that your library has the complete series before issuing the invitation. Check the official Web site of the series; often series' Web sites contain games, downloadable bookmarks, discussion questions, and other good stuff you might use before or during the Literary Lunch. Literary Lunches that highlight a favorite series tend to be very popular and full of energy.

Call attention to an overlooked series. There are always plenty of series that have waned in popularity but are still worthwhile of students' attention. A great way to drum up interest is to host a Literary Lunch that focuses on one of these series. Series such as Among the Hidden (Haddix), Time Warp Trio (Scieszka), or Boys Against Girls (Naylor) would work well for a Literary Lunch. Parents especially encourage their children to participate when the Literary Lunch focuses on a nostalgic series such as The Boxcar Children, Little House on the Prairie, Nancy Drew, or Encyclopedia Brown.

Select a theme. Often students who love a certain book will return to the library and ask for something "just like that other book." When multiple students begin to ask for similar kinds of books, give prominence to these kinds of reading patterns and suggest a Literary Lunch. Try topics such as books that make you cry, books about orphans, books written in verse, and books where kids travel in time.

Celebrate a holiday. Is Halloween coming up? Invite students to read a ghost story such as *The Dollhouse Murders,* by Betty Ren Wright. Is the winter solstice approaching? Gather together snow and winter stories. Would you like to acknowledge Presidents Day? Pull together biographies of U.S. presidents. Looking for an unusual way to highlight Black History Month? Select books that have won the Coretta Scott King award. Reading is always something to celebrate; a Literary Lunch can be a centerpiece of that celebration.

Once students come to understand how Literary Lunches work, expect them to offer their suggestions for topics for other Literary Lunches. You do not need to entertain their every wish, but use the opportunity to engage them in conversations about their ideas. Not only will you reinforce your interest in their reading, but you'll also gain insight into what the students are reading and thinking about. When students start requesting literary gatherings, consider it a strong sign that the reading culture in the school is taking hold.

How to Implement a Literary Lunch

Though Book Clubs and Literary Lunches are similar in that they pull together a community of readers, there are clear differences between them. Primarily, the participants at a Literary Lunch are reading different books, so rather than the discussion focusing on the same things, the conversation tends to be more of a sharing among students. Students take turns talking about what books they've read. Don't worry about facilitating intense discussion; rather, allow students the time and opportunity to talk about the different books. This might be the sweetest aspect of a Literary Lunch: students will hear about good books from other students, and they will take those recommendations seriously.

And just as you did with the student Book Club, you should allow time for the students to come in, get settled, jostle, talk, change their seat, and eat. Once students are settled, begin the conversation by having students introduce themselves and briefly tell what particular book they read that brought them to the Literary Lunch. This is important because the students need to have an understanding of the different titles available to them, and they will want to know if anyone else read the same book they did. You might ask the students if they notice any patterns in the reading choices, or ask if anyone read a book that was disappointing. Open the discussion up to the students and give them freedom to talk. You won't get the rhythm of a Book Cub, because you will have different students attending each Literary Lunch, but you will often get passionate responses as students defend or dismiss their books.

If a Literary Lunch is centered on a series, be prepared with some trivia questions about the series. Students attached to a particular series are often unabashed in their loyalty; they will love a chance to show off their knowledge of the series. Ask general questions that are basic to any book in the series so that if a student has read only one book in the series, he will have as much chance to answer as the student who has read six book in the series. For the Alex Rider series (by Anthony Horowitz), for instance, you might ask questions such as the following:

- What is the name of Alex's hometown?
- How old is Alex?
- What is the name of the organization that uses Alex as a spy?
- Name a sport at which Alex excels.
- What is the name of the character who creates Alex's gadgets?
- Name one of the languages Alex knows.

A trivia game like this can be a simple five-minute activity where students just raise their hands to answer a question. Prizes are not important; rather, you are creating a fun situation in which all the members share a common knowledge of the same literary occurrence. Sharing common knowledge is a central component to a culture, and creating a culture of literacy is the reason for your Literary Lunch. You can write these questions yourself or check a series' Web site for possible questions. You might even ask that each student contribute one trivia question prior to the Literary Lunch, and you can select the best questions to ask.

Because you are gathering during lunch, and because food and books go together so well, it's often a good idea to provide a snack for students who attend the lunch. A delicious dessert can be the perfect way to end a Literary Lunch, and your students will think you are sweet to treat them.

Other Ideas for Literary Lunches

If you have a large space for hosting a Literary Lunch, consider inviting parents to join you during the course of the year. Inviting parents to participate in a parent/child Literary Lunch will allow the parents a glimpse into the literacy activities in your school, as well as encourage them to read alongside their child. Ask parents to read a book related to the Literary Lunch topic; they can read the same book as their child or select another suitable title. Give parents plenty of notice so they can make arrangements to join their child on the day of the Lunch.

Another Tip for Literary Lunches

Print the theme of the Literary Lunch on a large poster board and have the poster available as the students enter the library. Have students sign in, and post the sign in the hallway near the library as both a recognition to those who attended and an incentive for the next Literary Lunch. Take photos during the Literary Lunch to hang alongside the poster, as well as to include in your library photo displays (see chapter 5).

Use your creativity and provide a treat or prop or music that matches the topic. Hosting a ghost story Literary Lunch in October? Keep the lights low and play spooky music as students enter. Having a Literary Lunch on a pirate theme? Ask everyone to wear a bandana. Make paper eye patches and play seafaring music in the background. Are you basing a Literary Lunch around the books of one author? Do some research into the author's life and serve a favorite food of the author's; not only will the students enjoy the treat, but it might spur an interesting discussion of the author and the author's books.

The possibilities for Literary Lunches and related activities are almost endless; they are limited only by the thousands and thousands of reading choices available to your students.

CALDECOTT BOOK CLUB

Book Clubs are necessarily designed for students who are independent readers, so most Book Clubs tend to be for third grade students and older. Ironically, some of the most enthusiastic readers in a school are those who are not yet independent readers, or perhaps not quite ready for chapter books. These students would love to belong to a library Book Club created just for them. And since the Caldecott Medal is awarded to the most distinguished picture books published each year in the United States, a Book Club centered on these beautiful books makes sense for these most enthusiastic young readers.

What Is a Caldecott Book Club?

A Caldecott Club is a perfect group for second graders, though just about all students, no matter their ages, could find things to discover and appreciate in these distinguished picture books. A Caldecott Club operates much like a Book Club for older readers, except that each student selects a different Caldecott Award–winning book each month. Students read their selected Caldecott book several times over the course of the month, and then prepare a drawing or an art piece to share with the group at the monthly Caldecott Club meeting.

How to Plan a Caldecott Book Club

The first thing you should do is make sure your students are aware of what the Caldecott Award is and why it is important. Even if students are not participating in a Book Club, the Caldecott Award is significant enough that every elementary student in the United States should be introduced to the books that are honored by this award. There are a wealth of lessons surrounding the Caldecott Medal, and the lessons could be taught both in the library and in the classroom. Be certain that students learn the difference between the gold medal and the silver medal, as well as the various media in which book illustrators work. Collaborate with the school art teacher for demonstrations about various art techniques used in award-winning books.

Invite your targeted group of students to join the Caldecott Club with verbal invitations as well as written invitations so parents are informed about the club (see Figure 3.5). Encourage the students to read and re-read their selected Caldecott book with their parents during the month so that they know their book well. Make sure students know that this library club is special, because in addition to reading books and talking about books, students will also create a picture based on their selected Caldecott book.

Help students learn to locate the Caldecott books in your collection. Some libraries gather Caldecott Award–winning books in a separate section of the library; other libraries keep the books on the regular shelves. Many libraries use a special spine label to indicate if a book has won a Caldecott Award. This helps patrons easily find these books on the shelves. A simple red star on the spine can also identify a Caldecott book. It is a good idea to have students verify with you whether a book has actually won a Caldecott Award. There are multiple awards given out to children's books, and students can easily mistake any gold or silver label as a Caldecott.

Because the Caldecott Award is based on the artwork of a book, part of each Caldecott Club meeting will be devoted to sharing the students' own artwork. Students must know what is expected of them regarding their art piece. The simplest requirement would be a colorful drawing on construction paper representing their favorite part of the story. Make sure students know that a different art project is required for each Caldecott Club meeting and that students must do their very best work on their drawing. Over the course of the school year, you might encourage students to explore a variety of art techniques, including black-and-white drawings, watercolor, colored pencil, paper cutouts, and so forth. An art teacher's involvement in a Caldecott Club project could be a wonderful ongoing collaborative effort, and a way to tie literature and art together in a significant way.

2nd Grade Caldecott Club!

The Caldecott Medal is an award given each year to the most distinguished picture book for children. 2nd graders are invited to join the library's Caldecott Club to read and learn about all the wonderful books that have won this important award.

Each month, 2nd graders are invited to select a Caldecott book from the school library. Students will take home their books to read and share with their families, and then create a beautiful picture based on their Caldecott books. The library will provide each child with a special piece of paper for the picture. Students can use colored pencils or paints or watercolors to make their picture.

During library class, we will talk about the different kinds of art techniques the book illustrators used to create their artwork. We will also give lots of suggestions to students for making a beautiful picture.

We will meet once a month in the library to discuss the Caldecott books. During the meeting, students will have a chance to share their books and their artwork. We will share dessert and drinks, too!

Each month, we'll put the Caldecott Club's artwork together to create a large CALDECOTT QUILT in the school hallway by the 2nd grade door. The first meeting is on Friday, October 17 at recess.

We hope each 2nd grader will join us!

Figure 3.5: Sample flier for a Caldecott Club.

From *Creating a Culture of Literacy: Programming Ideas for Elementary School Librarians* by Anne E. Ruefle. Santa Barbara, CA: Libraries Unlimited. Copyright © 2009.

How to Implement a Caldecott Book Club

Because these students are probably younger than those in a typical Book Club, keep the meetings simple. Meet during recess or after school so that you don't have to contend with lunch, and just offer lemonade and a light treat at the conclusion of the meeting. After students are gathered in your meeting spot, everyone will need an opportunity to share their book and corresponding artwork. Ask students to show their selected book, announcing the title and the author's name, and give them enough time to talk about the book. Ask students to briefly explain the story and possibly describe any art techniques they recognize. Modeling a sample presentation will help the young students understand what is expected. Be prepared to ask questions to help the students elaborate:

- Did you share your book with anyone at home?
- Do you have a favorite picture in the book?
- Have you read any other books by this author or illustrator?
- How do you think the illustrator created the pictures for the book?
- Why do you think this book won such a special prize?
- Why did you decide to make this particular picture to share with the Caldecott Club?

After students have a chance to talk about the book, they should share the pictures they created that are based on the book (see Figure 3.6). One

Figure 3.6: Students posing with their Caldecott creations.

of the most important aspects of a Caldecott Club, besides being a terrific vehicle for studying the Caldecott Award, is the students' artwork. Being able to respond to literature is vital in the development of a reader, and producing art based on a book is a powerful way to respond to a text. Make sure this artwork is prominently displayed after each meeting so that the larger school community can see the work these readers are doing. Create a Caldecott Gallery on an available wall, and hang up the pictures on a rotating basis throughout the year. Try a Caldecott Quilt and group the pictures together to form a large quiltlike mural on a wall. Bind all the pictures together and make a "Caldecott Book" that can be shared by every person who visits the library.

Other Ideas for a Caldecott Book Club

As the school year progresses, your students will become more comfortable not only with Caldecott books but also with the criteria used to select an award-winning book. Build on their knowledge by participating in a mock Caldecott celebration. Contact the local public library to see if it is organizing a mock Caldecott and ask if your students may participate. If you cannot locate a mock Caldecott celebration in your area, organize your own during the month of January by gathering together several dozen new picture books and asking students to vote on their favorites. Match your selections with those of the actual Caldecott committee once the formal announcements are made. You and your students might be able to watch the live podcast of the actual announcements via the ALA Web site; expect your students to cheer wildly if their selections match those of the Caldecott committee.

Another Tip for a Caldecott Book Club

If you have any new paperback picture books to distribute, put all the names of the Caldecott Club members in a hat and award a book or two at the conclusion of each meeting. Your students will love the anticipation of possibly winning a free book, and you will have found another way of getting books into the hands of students.

Finally, if the Caldecott Club goes well in your school and students are readily participating, you can easily transfer all of this information into the creation of a Newbery Club. Your students can graduate from a Caldecott Club to a Newbery Club, and their experiences with good books will continue to expand and deepen.

Chapter 4

Celebrating with Literary Events

Energetic Literary Programming
That Celebrates Both Readers and Books

A literary event is a special celebration that centers on literature. It is typically an event that is in response to something exciting happening in the world of children's literature: the 100th birthday of a beloved author; the 30th anniversary of a cherished book; a premiere of a major movie based on a favorite children's book; the publication of a much-awaited sequel. When an exciting literary occasion is imminent, you and your students will more than likely hear the buzz. Depending on the occasion, you'll notice posters in bookstores, read about it in blogs, see previews in the movie theaters, or hear about it at conferences. This chapter provides suggestion for ways to acknowledge those occasions. There is always something to celebrate in children's literature, and your responses to those occasions are the basis for literary events.

Literary Event @ the Movies
Library Lock-In
Library Sleepover
Literary Birthday Celebrations

LITERARY EVENT @ THE MOVIES

Hollywood has discovered what librarians have known for decades: children's literature is full of incredible stories. *Harry Potter; Twilight; The*

Tale of Despereaux; Holes; The Spiderwick Chronicles; The Dark Is Rising; A Series of Unfortunate Events; The Lion, the Witch and the Wardrobe; Inkheart; and *The City of Ember* are just some of the titles that have made it to the big screen in recent years. When a book of significant worth comes to a theater near you, consider hosting a field trip to a local theater for students who have read the book.

What Is a Literary Event @ the Movies?

A field trip to the local movie theater might not be the most conventional academic field trip, but it is certainly a worthwhile and extremely popular literary event. A Literary Event @ the Movies provides an opportunity for a group of students, all of whom have read the book, to attend a movie based on that book. The Literary Event @ the Movies typically takes place during a school day, though it could be arranged as an after-school event as well.

Advantages to taking students to the theater at the time of the movie's initial release, rather than waiting for the movie to be released in a DVD format, are threefold. First, you reach the students when the excitement is greatest. The marketing for the movie will also be marketing for the *book*; movies are wonderful, but you want kids to *read*—strike while the iron is hot. Second, by taking students to the movie theater, you do not have to worry about violating any potential copyright laws by viewing a DVD in a public performance setting. Finally, as every kid can attest, the popcorn is better!

How to Plan a Literary Event @ the Movies

Begin with a discussion with school administrators to determine the feasibility of a field trip to the movies. Because critical viewing and reading and comparison of different media are part of most language arts curriculums, a field trip to the movies isn't frivolous, but can be grounded in content standards.

Next, contact the theater. Find out if a school group can be accommodated, and don't hesitate to ask for a group or school discount. Once you understand the limits set by the theater, decide how many students you can take and how many other adult chaperones you will need. Enlist parents as well as teachers to accompany you on this field trip.

The movie that you are going to see will determine the age of the students you invite. Clearly, some movies are made for middle grade students, while other movies will be great for third and fourth graders. Obviously, pay attention to the movie's rating to help make this determination. In addition, view the trailers for the movie, often available months before the release date, to assess the appropriateness of the movie for your intended audience. As long as you are very familiar with the content of the book, you should have a pretty good sense of whether the movie will be appropriate for your students.

Advertise to the students a chance to attend a special Literary Event @ the Movies (see Figure 4.1). Emphasize that participation in this event is dependent upon students reading the book *before* they attend the movie. In this way, the Literary Event @ the Movies acts as both an incentive and a reward; students will try to read the book in order to attend, and they will be rewarded by seeing a movie because they read the book. As mentioned with a Literary Lunch (see chapter 3), you need some way to determine whether a student has actually read the book. You might ask students a series of questions about the book, or you might rely on your school's computerized testing programs. Students will need a clear deadline for completing the book, and parents need to be informed as to your expectations regarding reading deadlines, as well as costs for the movie and transportation requirements.

Because students will want to get their hands on the book, try to secure as many copies as possible. Reserve copies at the public library for your students to use. Check with local bookstores to see the price of a paperback copy of the book. Remember that if a movie based on a good book is forthcoming, kids all over the place will be vying to get their hands on a copy of the book. So, the earlier you get your students excited, the more likely they will be to find a copy and start reading.

How to Implement a Literary Event @ the Movies

Implementing a Literary Event @ the Movies will necessitate all the arrangements involved with a typical field trip: securing permission to take students off campus, preparing permission forms, determining costs, and arranging for chaperones and transportation. In addition to making these kinds of arrangements, make sure students have time to discuss the movie and the book as soon as possible after seeing the movie. Immediately after the movie, expect the theater lobby to be filled with students passionately talking about the movie. Though that initial discussion will be heated and fun, a more in-depth discussion comparing the film with the book is necessary. Students are often extremely possessive about the book and will not tolerate any deviations from the story the movie may offer. That's why a more formal discussion is vital; students should move from a simple discussion that centers on obvious differences between the book and the movie to a thoughtful dialogue regarding how different media approach a story.

Seen any good books lately?

You've read the book, now see the movie!

Mrs. Wickham's class and the library
have teamed up for a special field trip
to see
Charlotte's Web,
the film based on the book
on Friday, May 24.

After watching the movie, we"ll return
to school to have a discussion
comparing the book and the movie.

All permission slips need to be turned in by May 20.
Remember, you must first READ the book before you can attend the field trip.

Figure 4.1: Flier for Literary Event @ the Movies.

Depending on the number of students, as well as your schedule and resources, it can be fun to begin the dialogue over pizza right after viewing the movie. If that's not a possibility, gather all the participating students in the library or a large classroom the day after the movie for a group discussion. Venn diagrams or other graphic organizers can help facilitate this discussion. As students exchange ideas and debate the film, ask questions that lead toward critical thinking about different media:

- What are the obvious similarities between the movie and the book?
- What are the obvious differences?
- What has been added to the movie that isn't in the book?
- What aspects of the book were eliminated from the movie version?
- Why might a filmmaker change certain aspects of the movie?
- What might a movie do better than print?
- What might a book do better than a movie?
- What changes in the movie improved the story?
- What changes in the movie weakened the story?
- What scene worked best in the movie? Why?
- If you could make the book into a movie, what aspects might you change? Why?
- What other books do you think could be made into a good movie?

As students debate their ideas, they will learn that movies and books, as distinct types of media, are necessarily different. A discussion of the similarities and differences between the book and the movie can foster the complex, critical thinking that is a central goal of literate students.

Other Ideas for a Literary Event @ the Movies

Instead of offering a Literary Event @ the Movies to a large group of students, collaborate with a few teachers to take just a class or two of students. Because movie premieres are announced months in advance, it would be possible to acquire copies of the book and arrange for those classes to study the book in their language arts classrooms. You would be reassured that the students would be studying the book in-depth with their teachers, and they would be prepared to watch the movie with a critical eye. In addition to the manageable number of students for the field trip, collaborating with the teachers with shared lessons will offer a great opportunity to connect the library to the classroom.

Concentrating on just a class or two limits the number of students who might attend, but it is possible to go in the other direction and plan to take *everybody* in the school. Occasionally, a movie such as Paramount Pictures' 2006 *Charlotte's Web* appeals to audiences of every age. When planning a

Literary Event @ the Movies for the entire school, consider the size of your school, the accommodations of the local theater, the willingness of your staff, the cost for students, and the availability of transportation. If a movie that is based on a book is particularly well done, an all-school field trip can be an exciting and worthwhile literary event. Before going to see the movie, work with teachers to get copies of the book for each room. Depending on the length of the book, students could read the book as an assignment, or teachers could read the book aloud to their class. After the movie, each teacher would be responsible for conducting the discussions and facilitating any written responses or projects for the students regarding a book and movie comparison. Much like Breakfast with a Book or Same Book/Same Time (see chapter 2), an all-school event centered on a literary theme makes a powerful statement about the importance of literature in our lives.

Another Tip for a Literary Event @ the Movies

As with all your events, take photographs! Include a shot of students at the theater, perhaps in front of the marquee, holding copies of the book. Ask the theater for an extra movie poster to hang up in your library to promote your event. Check the movie's Web site to see if there are bookmarks, activities, or teacher resources to share. If students create any written or artistic responses to the book and movie, hang them up along with photographs from the Literary Event @ the Movies so the school community can share in the various student projects.

LIBRARY LOCK-IN

Students are often depicted in cartoons and TV sitcoms as lethargic and bored, slumped in their chairs, looking at the clock, and waiting for the school day to end so they can rush home to have fun. With some energy and planning of your own, you can reverse this picture and have children at home looking at their clocks after supper, desperately waiting until they can go back to school in the evening for a Library Lock-In!

What Is a Library Lock-In?

A Library Lock-In is an evening event where students come to school for a special night of reading-related games and activities, all centered around a particular theme or book or series. A typical Lock-In for students could be from 6:00 P.M. until 10:00 P.M., but those times can vary according to the age of the participants as well as your own schedule. Much as with a Literary Event @ the Movies, a Lock-In operates as both an incentive and a reward. Once you announce your criteria for a Lock-In, students work

Celebrating with Literary Events 69

hard to meet those requirements; if they meet the goal, they may attend the Lock-In. A Library Lock-In is a wonderful literary event, but here's a warning for you: once you host one, expect your students to clamor for more! Hosting one Lock-In a year is plenty, though, and your students will truly love it.

How to Plan a Library Lock-In

A Lock-In can be an intimate gathering of 12 students or a massive group of 50 or more. The size of the group is determined by the amount of space you have, the criteria you set, the expectations you have for the evening, and the number of additional chaperones you can convince to help you.

The most important part of a Lock-In is necessarily the literary aspect of the event. Carefully consider the criteria for students to attend. A Literary Lunch, as described in chapter 3, requires reading just *one* book in order to attend. But because you are investing considerable time and energy into an evening event, a Lock-In will require a bit more reading on the part of the student.

Possible reasons for a Lock-In might include the following:

- In honor of the publication of a new book in a popular series; students must have read the complete series or most of the series in order to attend.
- In honor of the anniversary of the publication of a popular book or series; again, students must have read the complete series or most of the series in order to attend.
- Successfully reading a challenging or difficult book (a book in the Redwall series by Brian Jacques, for instance).
- Students read a set number of Newbery books in anticipation of the annual Newbery announcement; schedule your Lock-In on the weekend proximate to the announcement.
- Celebration of a special event such as the completion of a library renovation or addition; invite the members of your Readers Hall of Fame to attend (see chapter 5).

Once you determine your criteria, it is time to set the date and issue the challenge for the Lock-In (see Figure 4.2). If you want students to read a complete series or read a set number of books for a Lock-In, allow ample time for students to reach that goal. You might schedule your Lock-In for the end of the year, but announce your challenge at the beginning of the school year. Providing an extracurricular year-long reading goal for students can be a wonderful byproduct of a Lock-In challenge.

Hear Ye! Hear Ye!

All you brave reading warriors are challenged to attend a

REDWALL Lock-In

in celebration of the publication of the newest book in the series by Brian Jacques.

If you decide to attempt this quest, you must read the first two books published in the Redwall series:

Redwall

and

Mossflower

(You may find copies of both books in our library and at the public library.)

Those brave souls who are successful in their reading quest may attend the REDWALL lock-in on Friday evening, November 7,

6:00 P.M. until 10:00 P.M.

Enjoy a Redwall Feast:
October ale, honey cakes,
goatsmilk cheese,
cabbage stalks, and hazelnuts!
(or choose lemonade,
chips and salsa,
chocolate chip cookies and
fresh fruit!)

See more details about the
lock-in on the library website.

Figure 4.2: Sample invitation to a Lock-In.

From *Creating a Culture of Literacy: Programming Ideas for Elementary School Librarians* by Anne E. Ruefle. Santa Barbara, CA: Libraries Unlimited. Copyright © 2009.

Do not overlook the importance of food for the evening, as the Lock-In is both a social and literary gathering. You might ask each family to contribute a food or drink item to share, or you could possibly order pizza for the group. Expect that after each group activity, students will flock to the food tables to eat and laugh and relax.

How to Implement a Library Lock-In

The activities you plan for the evening will depend on the ages of the participants and will center on the literary theme of your Lock-In. The Lock-In is designed to be fun and is not a classroom situation, so allot time for talking, eating, and independent activities in addition to planned activities. Begin with an icebreaker. Even if all the students know one another, a ritual beginning to the evening helps sets the tone and establishes a connection among the students.

A fun icebreaker is an FSW (Find Someone Who) game. Pass out a list of questions and ask students to find someone who can provide answers to the questions (see Figure 4.3). A game such as this gets the students up and moving, forces them to interact with other students, and intersperses the literary element throughout the icebreaker.

If you are working with younger students, you might take a look at the resource *Find Someone Who: Introducing 200 Favorite Picture Books,* by Nancy Polette. Students can use the Find Someone Who questions in this book to interact with other children while concentrating on specific picture books.

After the icebreaker, go right into another game. You might try Literary Charades. Have idea cards with book titles ready for the students, but allow students to act out their own suggestions as well. If your Lock-In is focused on Newbery books, have all the Charades idea cards list Newbery Award–winning books. Even if students haven't read all those books, they most likely will recognize the titles. After these two activities, open up the food table and give students time to eat and talk and relax. Break up the evening into sections of planned activities and open times to hang out. Not every activity has to be related to the literary aspect, and not every activity has to be a group activity. Students can choose to play a card game or play a popular group game such as Apples to Apples or Scattergories. If your space has the capabilities, you might even give students a chance to play video games or a Wii, but make sure students know that the electronic games are just *part* of the evening's activities.

Another good group game to play is a literary version of the old parlor game 20 Questions. Prepare cards with the names of well-known characters from popular books, one card for each student. Tape a card to the

FSW Game

For this activity, you must **F**ind **S**omeone **W**ho can answer the questions listed.
If you **F**ind **S**omeone **W**ho fits the question, get your paper signed next to the question.

Here's the tricky part: you can only have each person sign your paper just ONCE.
And you are NOT permitted to sign your own paper.
In other words, you have to keep on moving and talking to everybody in order
to complete your paper.

There are 25 questions listed – the first person to get 15 different signatures from
15 different people is the winner!

1. FSW was born in a different state
2. FSW has an older brother
3. FSW is a twin
4. FSW is allergic to peanut butter
5. FSW has read all seven Harry Potter books
6. FSW has a younger sister
7. FSW has read at least five Magic Tree House Books
8. FSW has been to Disneyworld
9. FSW plays at least two musical instruments
10. FSW is new to our school this year
11. FSW came to last year's library lock-in
12. FSW was in the Readers Hall of Fame last year
13. FSW knows how to ride a horse
14. FSW is a vegetarian
15. FSW wears glasses
16. FSW plays on a soccer team
17. FSW is in the Friends of the Library Club
18. FSW who has been to Washington D.C.
19. FSW knows another language besides English
20. FSW has a birthday in the same month as you
21. FSW has had a broken arm
22. FSW has read at least one Nancy Drew book
23. FSW knows how to water ski
24. FSW has never been in a plane
25. FSW has read *Eragon*

Figure 4.3: Sample "Find Someone Who" icebreaker game.

back of every student, and instruct the students that they may ask only "yes" or "no" questions to the other students in order to identify the name on their backs. Students can go one at a time, asking questions to the entire group, or everybody can play at once for a frenetic 20 Questions. Encourage students to ask questions such as the following:

- Am I male?
- Am I old?
- Am I a teenager?
- Am I part of a series?
- Do I have a best friend?
- Am I a main character?
- Am I a hero in the story?
- Do I have a family?
- Do I have any interesting physical characteristics?
- Am I an animal?

If your group is small and you are familiar with the reading habits of your students, you might select a character's name from a specific book that you know a student has read and loved. If that is not possible, there are plenty of popular book characters that virtually every student will recognize: Goldilocks, Captain Underpants, the Big Bad Wolf, Waldo, the Very Hungry Caterpillar, Harry Potter, Viola Swamp, Charlotte, Curious George, and so on.

If your Lock-In is centered on a series, such as Redwall, Harry Potter, American Girls, or Little House on the Prairie, a terrific group game to play is ABSeries. This game works well with any number of students, as long as the students are all familiar with the series. Divide your students evenly into groups; you can have anywhere from two large groups to six smaller groups.

Make 26 index-size cards, each with a different letter of the alphabet. Give each group a stack of paper and pencils. Shuffle the 26 alphabet cards, and deal the cards evenly around to the groups. If there is an uneven number of cards, toss out the "difficult" letters, such as Q, V, X, and Y, until each group has an equal number of cards.

On the count of three, each group takes its stack of alphabet cards and begins to write down people, places, and items pertaining to the series that correspond to the letters they have received (see Figure 4.4). Allow about 15–20 minutes for this game. Students will huddle together in their groups, calling out suggestions, helping one another come up with words that seem elusive, and congratulating team members who recall a particularly difficult word. Even if the students do not know one another well, because they have all read the same series, they are connected by the language and vocabulary of the books. A common language is a basic component of a culture, and this ABSeries game, as well as the Lock-In itself, helps solidify a culture of literacy in your school.

When the time comes for the Lock-In to end, call together the students to gather their things and ask them to take five minutes to help clean up. Ask if anyone has any suggestions for another Lock-In theme, or ideas for games or activities to play at next year's Lock-In. Let them leave knowing that another literary event could be in their future, because there will always be more books to read.

Other Ideas for a Lock-In

You might consider including an art project or craft as an activity for the evening. A hands-on project that reflects the theme of the evening would be a good addition to the scheduled activities. Provide inexpensive T-shirts and a box of permanent markers and ask everyone to make an "I was at the Library Lock-In" shirt. Students could make bookmarks, decorate shoelaces, contribute to a mural, or make a simple pop-up book.

Lock-Ins can engage students even over the summer. Right before the end of a school year, issue a reading challenge for the students to complete over the summer break. If they complete their reading goal, invite them to a Fall Lock-In. This would be a great way to establish rapport with students at the beginning of the school year, and give you an opportunity to promote the library as a place full of vivacious, interactive programming right from the beginning of the school year.

Another Tip for a Lock-In

Combine a Literary Event @ the Movies with a Library Lock-In. Arrange the movie as an after-school event, and then come back to the school for the Lock-In. Eat dinner, discuss the movie, play a few games, and then go home.

LIBRARY SLEEPOVER

Kids love sleepovers. Sleepovers have almost become rites of passage for elementary students. Packing a sleeping bag, toothbrush, and teddy bear is great fun when traveling to a friend's house for the night. Imagine the excitement of packing all those belongings to spend the night *in the school*! A Library Sleepover can be many things: a reward for meeting a reading goal, a hilarious night of activities and reading games, and a chance to get to know your students better. It is not, however, an opportunity to get a good night's sleep—but that's half the fun!

Sample A-B-Series Game
for Redwall series by Brian Jacques

Students work in groups to brainstorm people, characters, items, places, animals, foods, events, and so forth which will match the letters they've received.

Group A has received the letters
B, J, O, and R

B
badger
Bull Sparra
Basil Staghare

J
Jacques

O
October Ale

R
Redwall
rats
river

Group C has received the letters
D, M, L, and C

D
duels

M
Martin
Mariel
Matthias
Mossflower
moles

L
Log-a-log

C
Cluney the Scourge
Cornflower
Chickenhound

Group B has received the letters
A, S, V, and W

A
abbey
ale
Asmodeus

S
Salamnadstron
sword
stotes

V
vermin
voles
viper

W
weasels
woodland
Warbeak

Group D has received the letters
F, G, T, and P

F
foxes
Foremole
forest

G
goatsmilk cheese

T
turnips
tails
traitors
tapestry

P
paws

Figure 4.4: Sample ABSeries game.

From *Creating a Culture of Literacy: Programming Ideas for Elementary School Librarians* by Anne E. Ruefle. Santa Barbara, CA: Libraries Unlimited. Copyright © 2009.

What Is a Library Sleepover?

A Library Sleepover is much like a Library Lock-In, with the important distinction that the students don't go home at 10:00 P.M.; instead, students bring along pajamas and sleeping bags and stay all night in the library or other school facility. It is probably best to collaborate with a teacher or two to invite just a class or two at a time for a Sleepover. In that way, students already know one another, the teachers are familiar with the students, and parents will be comfortable with the event. You will also need to arrange for enough faculty and parent chaperones to ensure a safe, fun-filled event.

How to Plan a Library Sleepover

Both a Lock-In and a Sleepover require that parents know the drop-off and pickup times; for a Sleepover, parents also need to know what students should and should not bring. Students need sleeping bags, some sort of pajamas, and possibly a contribution to the evening's snacks. (A toothbrush is a good idea, though perhaps not realistic!) Individual electronic devices or music devices are *not* permitted during the evening. Cell phones may be in a student's suitcase, but should not be out for calls or texting during the evening. Parents need to provide emergency contact information before they drop off their child(ren), and it doesn't hurt to remind them of the morning pickup time before they leave their son or daughter with you for the evening.

Though a Lock-In and a Sleepover are certainly similar, the criteria for hosting a Sleepover might be significantly different if you concentrate on inviting just a class or two. Consider the reasons why you might collaborate with a teacher for a Sleepover; there are countless scenarios for hosting a Library Sleepover for just a class or two:

- Perhaps the third grade classes have read all the Ramona Quimby books, by Beverly Cleary, and have become huge fans of the series. Schedule a Sleepover on or around April 12, the birth date of Beverly Cleary. Plan on serving applesauce and Fig Newtons, just as Ramona's mother offered in *Beezus and Ramona*.
- A fourth grade teacher believes her 25 students are extremely capable readers who need a special challenge. Dare the students to collectively read 625 books between October and April, and host a spring Sleepover if they reach that goal (25 students reading 25 books equals 625 books).
- A fifth grade class has read the first two books in the first Warrior series, by Erin Hunter. Offer a Sleepover to any fifth grader who reads four more Warrior books.

- Sixth graders are reading *Hatchet,* by Gary Paulsen, in their language arts classes. Offer a Sleepover to any sixth grader who reads four more Gary Paulsen books in 54 days (the number of days that Brian was in the wilderness in *Hatchet*).

Though any of these situations could just as easily be celebrated as a Lock-In, if you have the energy and you have other faculty members willing to assist for an overnight, why not host an event that will be truly memorable for students?

How to Implement a Library Sleepover

All the activities you might plan for a Lock-In can also be used for a Sleepover; you just need to arrange a few more activities to last for a longer amount of time. As you are working with classroom teachers to develop the criteria for the Sleepover, brainstorm ideas for literary activities that students can play during the Sleepover. Though not every activity needs to be connected to the books or series, students will respond to those activities with enthusiasm.

Remember to allow for free time in addition to planned activities. Some activities will be for the entire group, but others might involve just a handful of students at a time. You might incorporate Readers Theater throughout the evening, asking groups of students to take turns presenting a story. Bring along several Readers Theater anthologies and have stories already selected for students to share.

Another suggestion is to randomly ring a bell throughout the evening. As soon as the bell is heard, everyone must freeze. Shout out a trivia question based on a book, and call on the first person who raises her hand. If the question is answered correctly, everybody can "unfreeze." Everyone stays frozen, however, until the question is correctly answered. Anyone who moves before the "unfreeze" signal is called becomes part of the evening's cleanup crew. Take care to call on different students during the night so that the same student does not answer every single question. You might have simple prizes on hand to distribute for the literary trivia questions. Paperback books, of course, make the best prizes.

Make sure students are aware of the time schedule for the evening. You might want to announce early in the night that all activities will cease by 11:30 P.M. so that students have time to use the restroom and brush their teeth before getting into their sleeping bags for a midnight story. Of course, you could end the activities earlier or later, but as every lover of stories knows, there is something magical about midnight. How fun for the students to be in their pajamas, in their sleeping bags, in the school, listening to a story at the stroke of midnight!

After everyone is settled into their sleeping bags, it is time to read a bedtime story or two. Expect that some students will beg for ghost stories, but unless you are certain that not one child will have nightmares, stay away from scary stuff. Instead, select several nice, long folktales, the kind of stories that engross readers and are capable of calming listeners. Since you are presumably reading aloud after midnight, anticipate that a few students will be asleep before you get to the second page, while others will be wide awake and waiting for more.

Do not be surprised if you have to whisper "Shhhhhh! Settle down!" more than once as some still-excited students will have a hard time going to sleep. Be patient; eventually every student will fall asleep, and you can get a few hours of rest. Station chaperones around the perimeters of the students and near entrances and exits for added security and safety.

In the morning, have juice and donuts available as the students rouse themselves from sleep. All you need to do in the morning is instruct students to gather together their sleeping bags, shoes, and other personal items and wait for the arrival of the parents. As students share donuts and juice, ask them which Sleepover activities they liked best, or what ideas they might have for a future Sleepover. It is good to get their immediate feedback, though expect some sleep-deprived students to have less than enthusiastic responses!

Other Ideas for a Library Sleepover

Do not announce this ahead of time, but plan to give a prize to the first and last students to fall asleep; award the prizes at breakfast. Sleepovers are also great places to take candid photographs of students playing games, eating pizza, and settling into sleeping bags. Take at least one group shot of all the Sleepover participants and make copies to distribute to everyone as a memento of a memorable literary event.

Another Tip for a Library Sleepover

Occasionally, even rarely, you might want to host a Sleepover at which no one actually sleeps; instead, the goal is to stay awake all night *reading* (see Figure 4.5). The publication of the seventh and final book in the Harry Potter series was just such an occasion, but keep your eye on the world of children's literature. There will certainly be another blockbuster book published in a popular series, providing an opportunity to host an all-night reading marathon. All you will need are students ravenous for the book, copies of the book for everybody to read, and a whole lot of caffeine.

Figure 4.5: Students reading at a Library Sleepover.

LITERARY BIRTHDAY CELEBRATIONS

"Happy birthday to you! Happy birthday to you! Happy birthday dear Eric or Tomie or Beverly! Happy birthday to you!" Every culture celebrates birthdays in different ways; indeed, celebrations are one of the most unifying factors within a culture. In Brazil, children eat beautiful candies shaped like fruits and vegetables. In Korea, a small feast is given in celebration on the 100th day of a child's life. A flag is flown outside a house in Denmark to show that someone in the house is celebrating a birthday. In your school, important birthdays of beloved authors, or anniversaries of the publication of cherished books, can be acknowledged as yet another way to bring the school together for a literary occasion.

What Is a Literary Birthday Celebration?

A schoolwide birthday party for an author is neither difficult to organize nor likely to happen on a regular basis. In the event, however, that a special birthday of a special author is approaching, you can be prepared with a simple literary event to mark the occasion. In 2004, the 100th anniversary of the birthday of Theodor Geisel—Dr. Seuss—made national headlines. In 2007, the 50th anniversary of the publication of *The Cat in the Hat* received similar attention. Both occasions were worthy of celebration, and though the worldwide appeal of Dr. Seuss and his books might not be easily duplicated, there will be other prominent books and authors to celebrate. Taking the time to celebrate the birthday of an author or the anniversary of a book is a reminder that books are important to your school community.

How to Plan a Literary Birthday Celebration

Do not worry about maintaining a calendar to keep track of possible birthdays or anniversaries. Just staying attentive to the world of children's literature should be enough to keep you informed. Library journals, blogs, listservs, wikis, conferences, and Web sites will certainly take note of important occasions, and you can follow their lead when they mention upcoming events.

When such an occasion is imminent, it is time to throw a little party. Begin by making sure that your students are familiar with the author and his books. Check to see if any biographies about the author are available. You will want your collection to have copies of the author's books, and you might take this opportunity to replace any old, beat-up copies with a new copy. The public library can provide you with multiple copies of books if you require many copies to circulate throughout the school.

Create a party atmosphere in the library that will call attention to the book or author being celebrated. Use birthday wrapping paper to cover a bulletin board or to drape over a display table. Decorate with streamers and balloons. Wrap small boxes in birthday wrapping paper and place books on top of the wrapped packages.

A good source of information and material will be available from the Web site of the author's primary publisher; in fact, the publisher will most likely be the source of much of the information regarding an upcoming birthday or anniversary. Take advantage of all the free stuff the publisher offers: posters, bookmarks, coloring pages, and teacher resources.

How to Implement a Literary Birthday Celebration

Once your background work is done, make sure you promote the upcoming event. Inform families about the significance of the occasion via fliers and the school Web site. If your school has been presenting regular Breakfast with a Book readings (see chapter 2), and the author has a book that would work well before a group, incorporate this book into a reading.

On the actual celebration day, create a party mood in the school. Depending on the book or author being celebrated, you might ask students to dress up as memorable book characters for the day. Entice members of the staff to wear birthday party hats as students enter the building in the morning. During morning announcements, have a student read a special birthday message to the rest of the school.

Keeping in mind the policies of the school's food service program, find out if it is possible to invite students to have a cupcake during their lunch period, after the meal has been served. If you receive permission to distribute cupcakes to the students, ask parents a week or two before the date to send cupcakes for a schoolwide party. Make your expectations clear. Will you need 200 or 600 cupcakes, one for every child in the school? Decorate your cupcake tables and display any appropriate posters or pictures or books to make the cupcake tables festive and to remind the students why they are receiving this treat. It's up to you if you want to make the students sing "Happy Birthday" before passing out the cupcakes!

Other Ideas for a Literary Birthday Celebration

A schoolwide Birthday Celebration can be a great opportunity for you to implement a Same Book/Same Time (see chapter 2). If the author has a suitable book that could be shared with multiple grades, or if the special book is short enough to share, you have a perfect reason to arrange a schoolwide reading. A Same Book/Same Time could be done in anticipation of the upcoming birthday, or it could be done on the day of the actual celebration. Either way, it connects kids to the book.

Another Tip for a Literary Birthday Celebration

Enlist your Friends of the Library Club to help make a large birthday card or banner. Have it ready a week prior to the event so that every person in the school has time to sign the card. Hang your banner in the library or cafeteria or main hallway, along with book covers, biographical information, newspaper clippings, and anything else that will help highlight the reason for the birthday celebration. Make sure students understand that for this kind of party, no gifts are required. The author you're celebrating has already provided the best kind of gift to open.

Chapter 5

Involving the School Community

Yearlong, Ongoing Programming That Reaches Out to the School Community

In order to create a culture of literacy, every member of the school community needs to be included. This chapter provides ways in which families, students, faculty, and other stakeholders share in welcoming, recognizing, and rewarding readers. As these programs are woven into the fabric of your school, they serve to reinforce the culture of literacy within your school community.

Welcome New Readers
Birthday Book Program
Readers Hall of Fame
Newsletters
Scrapbooks and Photo Albums

WELCOME NEW READERS

There's nothing quite like the arrival of a new baby—such excitement, such joy, such sweetness. For a librarian it's particularly exciting, because it means another new reader has come into the world! A Welcome New Reader program is a simple yet powerful way for your library to begin developing relationships with the youngest members of the school community. Early literacy is fundamental to the development of a lifelong reader and learner. With the gesture of a new book for each new baby in your school community, the library reinforces the literacy connection between school and family.

What Is a Welcome New Reader Program?

Your library has the opportunity to establish a rapport with families every time a new sibling arrives in a school household, by presenting the family with a new book as a welcome gesture. Though your goal is to begin (or add to) a personal library for each child, parents will love to have their new addition acknowledged, older siblings will be thrilled to bring home a present for the little sister or brother, and the library will gently help a family begin the process of raising a reader.

How to Plan a Welcome New Reader Program

The process begins once you find out that a new baby has been born. Such announcements are common around elementary schools, as proud older siblings rarely contain their excitement about the birth of a new brother or sister. Now it is time to welcome the new reader.

Keep inexpensive gift bags on hand. Pink and blue bags are obvious, but plain white bags also work well, since they are easily decorated with baby stickers that can be found in stationery and craft stores. You can use these gift bags to put together a Welcome New Reader gift for the new baby.

Be on the lookout for books to distribute to babies. Plan on keeping a small stockpile of paperback or board books that are suitable for a baby. Keep these books in a special location so that they are ready once you hear the announcement of a new arrival.

Inside each book, place a bookplate or label with a message identifying the book as a gift from the library (see Figure 5.1). Labels or bookplates

Figure 5.1: Sample bookplate for a Welcome New Reader book.

can be created with any of the popular label-making or print shop programs available. Print at least 20 labels at the beginning of the year to have on hand as the need arises.

Depending on your stockpile, you might also include a bookmark, a pack of crayons, or a brochure from your state Department of Education regarding the importance of early literacy—anything that reinforces the idea of reading.

How to Implement a Welcome New Reader Program

If your school is small, it is possible that you will know when each new sibling is born to a school family. If your school is large, it could be virtually impossible to keep track of all the new arrivals. No matter what size school you serve, so that you do not overlook any new siblings, enlist the help of your faculty and school staff to inform you when a new baby is imminent. The school secretaries will be especially helpful. They often have the most information regarding the happenings in the school, and you could ask them to let you know about any new siblings so that the library can acknowledge the birth in a timely manner. Once the program is established and students know that the library distributes books to new babies, expect that proud big brothers and sisters will make sure you know when the baby arrives.

As soon as possible after hearing the good news, prepare a Welcome New Reader gift bag for the family. On the gift bag, write a bright, colorful message welcoming the baby, similar to the label pictured in Figure 5.2. If you are unsure of the spelling of the new baby's name, it's worth a phone call home. A seven-year-old big sibling might be the most enthusiastic family member but not necessarily the most reliable speller.

If possible, involve the older sibling in this process. If you have a collection of books for babies, ask the big brother or big sister to select the book for the gift bag. Let him or her watch as you write the baby's name on the bag. If there are stickers with which to decorate the gift bag, ask him or her to help stick these on the bag. Make sure that the big brother or sister is the one to deliver the gift bag to the new baby and that he or she understands the importance of reading as early as possible and as often as possible to the new baby!

Other Ideas for a Welcome New Reader Program

It can be expensive to provide a new book for every new baby in your school community. These don't have to be hardback books—your goal is to

Welcome, Nina Gabrielle!

Figure 5.2: Sample welcome message to a new baby.

simply acknowledge the birth. Keep a lookout for inexpensive baby board books during the year, purchasing two or three at a time. If you have a Book Fair at your school, acquire a dozen or so suitable paperback books for babies. Don't hesitate to ask your Book Fair company to donate a few books *specifically for this program*. Book Fair companies are in business to make a profit, but they also share in your goal of creating a literate society. Perhaps your parent-teacher organization might help fund a collection of books to use for the Welcome New Reader program. Keep your eyes open when you attend library conferences to pick up freebies that you can pass on to your families.

This is an ongoing program that truly resonates with parents. They will be delighted that the birth of their new baby is acknowledged, and they will be thrilled that the newest member of their family is considered to be a part of the larger school family.

It can be work to locate new, inexpensive, and appropriate books for the Welcome New Reader program, but keep in mind that this book might be the only book some babies will receive as a gift. Creating a culture of reading must extend to all members of the school community, including the newest arrivals.

Another Tip for the Welcome New Reader Program

Ask your school families with new babies to send in a photo of the new baby with the older siblings, and display the photographs together under a Welcome New Readers banner. Encourage the families to include a book in the photograph. Add new pictures all year long to create a collage of babies and books that is sure to charm every visitor to your library.

It is a great thing to start life
with a small number of really good books
which are your very own.

Sir Arthur Conan Doyle

BIRTHDAY BOOK PROGRAM

Everybody loves a birthday celebration—especially if you are an elementary-age student. Why not invite students to share their birthdays with the entire school community by donating a book to the library? Organize a Birthday Book program that not only offers a wonderful way to bring together books and children but also helps increase the library collection.

What Is a Birthday Book Program?

A Birthday Book program is a yearlong program where students are invited to celebrate their birthday with the school library by donating a book to the collection. Students and their families receive a personal letter during the month of the student's birthday, and the families decide whether to participate. A Birthday Book program can quickly become successful at your school by following these six basic steps:

1. Acquire the books
2. Invite the children to participate
3. Allow student to select the book
4. Label the book
5. Acknowledge the donation
6. Thank the family

How to Plan a Birthday Book Program
Acquire the Books

Before you invite the students to celebrate their birthday with a donation to the library, you'll need to make sure you have some wonderful book choices for them. It's best to begin by purchasing several dozen books.

Fully process and catalog the books, but *don't* put them out for circulation. These Birthday Books should be kept out of view of students, perhaps on a special shelf or in a decorated Birthday Box (a box wrapped with birthday wrapping paper works nicely). When a child is ready to select a book in honor of a birthday, he is invited to peruse the Birthday Box to make a selection.

The size of your enrollment as well as your budget will determine the number of books in your school's Birthday Box. Try to start with at least two dozen books—you'll want to make sure students have a wide variety from which to choose. As the books are depleted over the course of the year, add more books so the selection never falls below 20 or so books. If your school population is quite large and response to the Birthday Books is strong, you'll have to adjust how many books you keep on hand for your selection.

Select books that will appeal to a wide range of readers. If you have both primary and middle grades you'll need to make sure you have books for different reading levels. Look for high-interest books; dinosaur, snake, and animal books always seem to be favorite choices across the ages. Provide a variety of genres: fiction, nonfiction, history, and poetry. Books in popular series work well (Junie B. Jones, Diary of a Wimpy Kid, Magic Tree House, and so forth). Birthday Books are often a great place to gain a second or third copy of favorite titles for your library collection. Need a new copy of *Charlotte's Web, Harry Potter,* or *The True Story of the Three Little Pigs*? Offer some of these titles in your Birthday Box; students will love to select an oldie-but-goodie as their Birthday Book.

Invite the Children to Participate

The next thing to do is to *invite* each person in the building to celebrate her birthday by donating a new book to the library. Most schools now maintain a database of information about all of the children in the school. Ask for a list of all the birthdays, arranged in a monthly format. At the beginning of each month, send home a letter to each family who has a child celebrating a birthday that month, inviting the family to celebrate by donating a book to the school library. These letters can be mailed (which can get expensive) or given to each child to take home, or perhaps your school has a communication system in place (weekly folders or e-mail) by which parents receive information. Preparing and sending the birthday letters would be a wonderful project for a library volunteer.

The letter should explain your program, such as how much a Birthday Book donation will cost, and how the child will go about selecting a book (see Figure 5.3). Make sure your letter explains that the book *will remain*

Dear Family of _____ ,

"Happy Birthday to You! Happy Birthday to You!
Happy Birthday Dear Student,
Happy Birthday to You!"

As you are well aware, your child celebrates a birthday on _____ ,
and we are inviting you to celebrate your child's birthday by donating a book to our school
library. Your child may come to the library any day this month and select a brand new,
beautiful hardback book from our BIRTHDAY BOOK BOX. We'll put a special bookplate
in the front of the book that will announce to all readers of the book just who donated the
book to our library! *(See a sample bookplate below.)*

This book will become part of our permanent collection,
but your birthday child will be the very first person to check out the book!

If you'd like, you may send in your child's school photograph (or any photograph of your
choice), and we'll include that in the front of the book, along with the donation label.
The cost for any book in our Birthday Book Box is $15.00. If you are interested in
celebrating your child's birthday in this manner, please send a check or cash with your child
in a sealed and marked envelope.

Your generosity and thoughtfulness are much appreciated,
and you can be sure that this gift will be
shared and celebrated by all of our students
for many years to come.

Thank you!

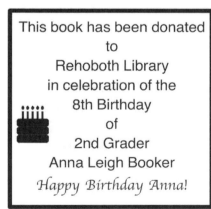

This book has been donated
to
Rehoboth Library
in celebration of the
8th Birthday
of
2nd Grader
Anna Leigh Booker
Happy Birthday Anna!

Figure 5.3: Birthday Book sample letter.

a permanent part of the collection, and that all children will have access to the book—though the birthday child will be the first person to check out the book.

Of course, you can't neglect those students who celebrate summer birthdays. Send home the June-July-August birthday letters in January or February (see Figure 5.4); those children will love anticipating their birthday months in advance.

Though children will be the focus of the Birthday Book program, why not also invite the faculty and staff to donate a book on their birthdays? The entire school community should share in the culture of literacy—especially when it comes to a celebration!

How to Implement a Birthday Book Program

Allow the Student to Select the Book

Once you send out the invitations at the beginning of each month, you just need to wait until a child arrives—usually clutching an envelope and sporting an ear-to-ear grin. Of course, you'll make a fuss over the child as you escort her back to the Birthday Box or shelf. Allow her to take as much time as she likes to select her Birthday Book. If your goal is to build a culture of literacy, then it's important for the student to feel as if this book is the most important book in the school.

Though most children will easily select a book from the 20 or more titles you provide at any given time, it is possible that some students will simply not be happy with your preselected books. On a case-by-case basis, you might inquire what kind of book the student wishes, and then look for a specific book or topic. In fact, some schools arrange all their Birthday Book donations in this manner: a student requests a book by title or topic, the librarian searches for a suitable book, and then it is added to the collection. That certainly is a plausible alternative—but it is also time consuming and perhaps more costly. If you receive 75–100 birthday requests in a school year in this manner, you will spend an inordinate amount of time shopping for individual requests. In addition, a student might have to wait several weeks before a suitable book is found, thereby postponing the birthday "celebration" and possibly diminishing his interest in the book. If you take the time to purchase at least two dozen high-interest, high-quality books at a time, you'll be able to please almost all your Birthday Book customers.

An alternative process might be to ask children to choose a book already in the collection. Students pick a title with which they are already familiar, and their birthday label is placed in that book. Another new book is then added to the collection with the new funds.

Dear Parent of Summer Birthday Child,

As you are well aware, _____ is one of those special children with a summer birthday. These "summer kids" are lucky enough to swim or sun on their birthday, but they also miss the opportunity of sharing their birthday with their classmates at school. At the school library, we don't want your summer child to be overlooked in our BIRTHDAY BOOK PROGRAM, and so that is why we're writing to you now.

Please find attached a copy of the letter we send to all the fall-winter-spring birthday children. If you'd like your summer-fun child to participate, we invite you to select ANY school day on which to celebrate a special "school year" birthday. Then, send in a check for $15.00 to the library, and we'd be delighted to have your child select a beautiful, brand new book that can be enjoyed throughout the school year by all of our students, including your special summer child!

Thank you!

Figure 5.4: Summer birthday letter.

From *Creating a Culture of Literacy: Programming Ideas for Elementary School Librarians* by Anne E. Ruefle. Santa Barbara, CA: Libraries Unlimited. Copyright © 2009.

Label the Book

Once a child selects a book, it's time to make sure the book is properly identified as a Birthday Book. Make this a fun ritual for the child donating the book. A suitable bookplate must go on the front end paper so that every person who reads this book will immediately see whose birthday the book celebrates (see sample in Figure 5.5). Birthday Book labels can

Sample birthday bookplate

Figure 5.5: Sample Birthday Book bookplate.

be easily created using simple label-making or print shop programs. You could also pay a printer to create a special Birthday Book label template, but it would cost more than using your own computer program.

In addition to the label, there are other possibilities to help identify the Birthday Book. Ask the family to send in a photograph of the child to be included along with the bookplate. It's a powerful way to make a child feel connected to a special book. The school office often keeps extra copies of school photographs; you could ask permission to use one of these. If you add photographs to the books, you can be sure students will love to hunt for the pictures of their friends inside the books.

Finally, it is a good idea to identify the Birthday Book by placing some sort of special label or sticker on the spine. You could use your handy paint/art/label program to create a special spine label. An easier way is to purchase candle stickers to place on the spine of each Birthday Book. Stickers shaped like candles can be found, rather inexpensively, at stationery stores, art and hobby shops, and scrapbook supply stores. The colorful candle stickers on the spines of dozens of books will certainly brighten the library shelves—much like that of the lit candles on a birthday cake!

Once the book is properly labeled as an official Birthday Book, the birthday child gets the privilege and honor of being the very first person to check out the book.

Other Ideas for a Birthday Book Program
Acknowledge the Donation

It's important to acknowledge every donation, no matter how small. In order to create a sense of importance and prominence to the Birthday Book, every donation can be announced by means of a special bulletin board. Perhaps the bulletin board can be made to look like a giant cupcake, and every time a book is donated, another candle is added to the cupcake. Another idea is to transform the bulletin board into a large birthday gift, adding a small "gift tag" with the name of the Birthday Book donor. The growing list of donors and books will both spark interest in the books and acknowledge the donors.

Thank the Family

Even if you take the time to label the books, display the books, and acknowledge the books, there is still one more step to take: you must thank the family. Writing thank-you notes is more than just good manners; it is a way to ensure that each family who donates a book understands that they are actively contributing to the reading needs of every child in the school. That is no small feat—and it needs to be addressed with a formal thank-you. Even if you use just a postcard or a form letter with a personalized signature, you will have gone a long way in thanking families for their generosity and their contribution to the reading culture of the school.

At the end of the year, every student who donated a Birthday Book could be invited to the library for a cupcake and juice as another way to say thanks.

Another Tip for a Birthday Book Program

As with most programs in the library, cost will be a consideration. Should the donation cover the entire cost of the book? This is a matter of some debate. Hardback books cost anywhere from $17 to $25; asking for that much money could prohibit many families from participating. It's probably best to ask for a standard donation to cover a portion of the cost of the book, while the school library pays the rest. In this way, there is really a sharing between the families and the library regarding the library collection. Asking for $10 or $15 will go a long way toward the purchase price of a book.

One issue to consider is that not all families can afford to participate in the Birthday Book program. Students whose families are able to make a donation will be delighted—students whose families cannot afford a Birthday Book will be disappointed. As with all things, handle such occurrences with diplomacy. If a child is disappointed that he cannot purchase a Birthday Book, reassure him that Birthday Books are for everyone and that it doesn't matter that his name isn't inside a book—he can check out any Birthday Book in the library. Books are for sharing—that's the most important message of a Birthday Book.

It is not unusual once the program becomes fully established for a family to donate money (often anonymously) so that a child from another family can select a Birthday Book. It can be amazingly rewarding to invite a child to select a Birthday Book because of the generosity of others. Some libraries may wish to set aside some acquisition funds to pay for Birthday Books for families who cannot afford to participate in the program.

Though the Birthday Book program can be successful in its very first year, once the program has been in place for several years you'll see its full impact. It is a great public relations tool for your library. Parents will like participating in the collection development, and students will feel a real connection to the books they and their classmates donate. There's nothing like watching a sixth grader hunt through the shelves to find the book she donated in kindergarten, or hearing a visiting alumnus ask if the *Captain Underpants* book he donated in second grade is still on the shelf. The typical child's birthday party is over in two hours, and most of the gifts fade away after a month or two. A book donated to the library, however, can last well over a decade. Dozens and dozens of readers will share Birthday Books—and that's something to celebrate.

READERS HALL OF FAME

Enter nearly any high school in America and you will see portraits of the school's premier athletes lining the hallways: state champions, all-Americans, all-state award nominees, and school record breakers. These hallways of champions are testimonies not only to the athletes but also to the athletic departments—the world of athletics does an extraordinary job of promoting and congratulating itself. The world of literacy could take a lesson from the wide world of sports.

Wouldn't it be incredible to enter a school and find a hallway lined with photographs of the school's most accomplished readers? That's exactly what you can do with a Readers Hall of Fame wall.

What Is a Readers Hall of Fame?

A Readers Hall of Fame is a way to honor students who have distinguished themselves as outstanding readers. Students become members of the Readers Hall of Fame if they meet the criteria your school has determined. Once students reach this goal, their pictures are taken and hung up in a visible area of the school. A Readers Hall of Fame typically will be a wall sporting a collection of colorful 8 × 10 pictures of students, each student posing with a favorite book. During the course of the school year, the Hall of Fame should regularly have photographs added to it as more and more students reach their reading goal. Digital cameras and color copiers make such a wall an easy possibility. The more difficult issue is to determine the criteria for students to reach the Readers Hall of Fame. With a little collaboration, a little bit of money, and a little encouragement, you can begin a Readers Hall of Fame that will be a true testimony to some real champions.

How to Plan a Readers Hall of Fame

The first thing to do is check with administrators to determine the feasibility of beginning such a program. Assuming that your administrators see the value of recognizing the accomplishments of the readers in your school, they will embrace and encourage the idea. Next you will need to approach the teaching staff, particularly those individuals who teach reading and literature.

After describing a potential Hall of Fame wall, you will need to lead a discussion with all interested parties to determine the criteria by which a student might be included. At this point you'll need to demonstrate your collaboration skills. There are certainly many options, ranging from teacher nominations to students passing some sort of test. Try to strike a balance when deciding on the criteria. On one hand, the standard should be manageable, but on the other hand, the goal should be set at a level that requires students to exert extra effort in order to achieve it. Creating a culture of literacy is based on the principle that all of us need to be lifelong readers and learners; you want to encourage reading, not exclude readers. Having said that, you still need to have a goal for readers to work toward so that the Hall of Fame is not considered "ho-hum."

Many schools participate in computerized reading/testing programs, such as Accelerated Reading or Reading Counts. If your school currently uses any of those types of programs, you have a built-in system already in place. Perhaps every student who reaches 100 points (or another such number) could be considered a member of the Readers Hall of Fame. Perhaps every student fifth grade and older who reads a certain number of books (25? 30? 40?) might enter the Readers Hall of Fame. Many literature classrooms use Literature Circles or Reading Journals as part of their everyday curriculum; classroom teachers can suggest ways to use the information gathered in classroom settings as a way to determine eligibility for inclusion in a Readers Hall of Fame.

Not every grade level need have the same criteria. Whatever criteria are deemed appropriate, however, must be clearly explained to the students as well as their parents. After determining the criteria, advertise to your students the Readers Hall of Fame. Be sure to give the Hall of Fame suitable fanfare; prepare a "marketing blitz" so that students are excited about the possibility of being a member of the Readers Hall of Fame. After your first year of implementing a Readers Hall of Fame, you will not need to market as much, because the previous year's Hall of Fame will stand as a testimony to the glory of your school's reading!

How to Implement a Readers Hall of Fame

Once a student is determined eligible for the wall, the student should receive some official notification that, due to her outstanding reading, she has become a member of the school's Readers Hall of Fame. Next, the student will need a picture taken. The student should select a favorite book for the picture. If the book is covered in clear plastic, ask the student to tilt the book forward to avoid glare on the book cover. Take care to select an appropriate background for the photo, as the background provides the atmosphere of the poster. With a digital camera, you have the luxury of taking multiple photographs in order to get one good picture. The photographer and the subject should agree on the best picture (which is not always easy when the subject of the photo is 12 years old!).

If you are ambitious, the desired photograph is sent to your Print Shop program so you can add a name, date, and title. If you want to go an easier route, simply print out the photograph, mount it on construction paper, and label it with similar information (name, date, title of favorite book; see Figures 5.6 and 5.7).

ALA Graphics currently has software for creating photographs similar to its famous celebrity READ photos. Your Readers Hall of Fame wall could be filled with students' READ photos. This requires the extra step on the computer of using photo editing software to remove the background from the photo and replace it with one of the backgrounds provided on the ALA Graphics CD. If you plan to edit the photo in this way, you may want to photograph the student in front of a solid background. This will help when you remove the background of the photo.

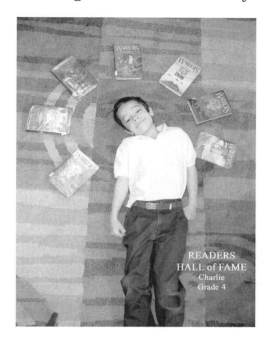 

Figure 5.6 and 5.7: Sample Readers Hall of Fame photographs.

How you handle the photographs will certainly depend on the resources and technology available at your school. You might be able to print out 8 × 10 color photographs easily, or 4 × 6 might be your limit. If 4 × 6 is your standard, you might consider enlarging the photo to an 8 × 10 on a color copier (if your school does not own one, you could take it to a copy store), making a copy for both the school hallway and the family of the reader. If your budget allows, you could make the photographs even larger than 8 × 10, but consider that the larger the enlargement, the greater the cost.

Though you are creating these photographs to display in a school hallway, plan on making a copy of the photograph for the family of the reader. It is an added expense, certainly, but worthwhile to imagine the delight of the family receiving the photograph, as well as the additional public relations boost your library receives from distributing photographs to the school families.

Remember to create a space in which to hang all of the Readers' photographs. Select a high-traffic area that is visible enough so that visitors can also see the photographs and understand the emphasis your school places on reading. Make a banner that proclaims READERS HALL OF FAME. As students' photographs are added to your Hall of Fame wall over the course of the year, expect to see other students regularly looking at the new photos, comparing pictures, noticing what books are depicted, and proclaiming that they, too, will one day soon be part of the Readers Hall of Fame.

Other Ideas for a Readers Hall of Fame

Though students who become members of the Readers Hall of Fame gain the respect of their peers, the admiration of the faculty, and the loyalty of their librarian, as well as the honor of their photograph lining the hallowed halls of academia, your school may wish to supply an additional reward for induction into the Readers Hall of Fame.

If your school has an honors assembly of any kind, students recently added to the Readers Hall of Fame could be acknowledged during the assembly. Remember the analogy of the athletic departments? Athletic banquets with trophies and plaques and ribbons are standard fare, so a mention at a school honor or recognition assembly would certainly be a reasonable acknowledgment for the readers' achievements.

You might host a quarterly or annual gathering of Readers Hall of Fame students. Depending on the number of students (not to mention your budget), you could have a pizza party, a special Literary Lunch (see chapter 3), or just cake and punch to say "Congratulations" to your school's hard-working, dedicated readers.

Another Tip for a Readers Hall of Fame

At the end of the year, the photographs come down and the Readers Hall of Fame will begin anew the following school year. You might save the photographs for placement in a scrapbook devoted just to Readers Hall of Fame photographs.

You might also use all the photographs you've created as screen savers in your library or the school's computer lab. Students will be thrilled to see themselves and their classmates posted as screen savers, and the visibility of the Readers Hall of Fame will be yet another reminder of the importance of reading.

NEWSLETTERS

You do amazing things in your library every day, but are you certain your school community really knows what you do or what's happening in the library? Advocacy for school libraries doesn't just mean lobbying Capitol Hill or writing to your state senators or even negotiating with your own administration. According to the ALA Public Awareness Committee, advocacy is "turning passive support into educated action by stakeholders . . . advocacy is an umbrella that includes public relations and public awareness." (*American Libraries*, "Advocacy Grows @ Your Library," vol. 35, p. 32, February 2004). In other words, while it is essential for libraries to work toward advocacy on large-scale political fronts, it is also essential to advocate on a smaller scale, including your own school community, with something as simple as a newsletter.

What Is a Newsletter?

Newsletters are wonderful public relations tools. A newsletter works as a summary of events, a glimpse into the statistics that drive the library, and a way to introduce or describe some of the major activities you are undertaking. Without too much effort on your part, newsletters can be a manageable, small-scale way to inform the school community of the many things happening within a school library.

A newsletter can go a long way toward educating students, parents, faculty, school board members, and community stakeholders about various aspects of the school library. Don't think of newsletters as "blowing your own horn"; rather, consider newsletters as a way to educate the school community about details they might otherwise miss.

How to Plan a Newsletter

Newsletters shouldn't be painful to write, nor should they be long-winded. A one- or two-page newsletter is more than adequate. A newsletter works well once or twice a year—perhaps written and distributed at the conclusion of each semester. It's important that as many stakeholders as possible receive a copy of the newsletter. Parents, of course, should receive a copy, as well as your local administration, school board members, representatives in your district office—anyone who is significant to your school community.

Consider how your newsletter will be distributed. Mailing individual copies, even a one-page document, could be very expensive. Plan so that your newsletter is included in a mass mailing the school has already scheduled. Or, if your school or district distributes information to families via mass e-mail, make arrangements for your library newsletter to be distributed in the same way. Posting your newsletter electronically on your school's Web site is a must; the advantage of posting a newsletter is that it remains visible to the public for a much longer time, and your library activities will continue to get the attention they deserve every time someone visits that Web site.

How to Implement a Newsletter/Possible Items to Include in a Newsletter

The most difficult aspect of writing a newsletter is knowing what to include. Try some of these suggestions for an assortment of ideas that can be adapted for your own newsletter.

Interesting statistics. Do your families know the number of circulated volumes during the year? At the end of a school year, parents and staff alike will be astounded at how many books were checked out—and shelved—during the course of one year. If your circulation program can provide you with various reports, you might be able to determine which book, according to circulation statistics, is the most popular book in the library. Let your school community know the Top 10 Favorite Books of your school. Do you know how many volumes you hold in the library? Let your school community know. Not only are you providing interesting statistics, you are reminding newsletter readers that the library is a dynamic environment. Further, if you are fortunate enough to have a support staff, this information can provide data to justify the need for the additional help. These statistics can be a testament to the amount of work, by both paid staff and volunteers, that goes into running a library.

Number of Birthday Books added. You might individually list each child and the title of the book. Not only are you highlighting a child's birthday, you are also publicly acknowledging a donation—both of which are good things! It is also a good way to attract other parents to participate in the program.

Number of new books and other items added. Students constantly ask, "Do you have any new books?" There is something exciting about getting anything new—and since libraries share their "new" items with everyone, why not let the school community know just how many new items were purchased, processed, and catalogued during the school year. And if you add more than 180 items in the course of a year, you can point out that the library added something new for *every* day of the school year!

List any donations received. This is a good way to publicly acknowledge a donor, and it might also serve as a catalyst for someone else to consider making a donation to the library.

Collaborative projects between the library and a classroom or with a teacher. Effective school libraries collaborate with classroom teachers on an ongoing basis. Some projects are more noteworthy than others. Use the newsletter to remind the school community of the many ways school libraries impact student learning. Did the sixth grade work on a research project involving intellectual property rights? Did a group of third graders investigate biographies and make posters depicting their discoveries? Have fourth graders completed an author study? Include such successful projects in your newsletter.

Recognition of the Friends of the Library Club. Let your school community know how the Friends Club (see chapter 3) has helped out in the Media Center. Recognize the students' efforts while reminding parents what a busy place the library continues to be.

Updates on Book Clubs, Literary Lunches, and other literary events. Don't assume that the entire school community knows about your activities working with students. This is your chance to highlight these activities while possibly enticing other students to participate in upcoming events. How many students were in your Book Club? What novels did you read? Did your students read a novel and then see a matching film for a side-by-side comparison? This is your chance to tell the school community.

Did you host a Lock-In? Did the intermediate grades celebrate the birthday of Beverly Cleary? Did the second graders participate in a mock Caldecott? All you need are a few sentences to inform your readers of the myriad of activities that take place in your library.

Book Fairs. Book Fairs are anticipated events at many school libraries. Use the newsletter to let your school community know how much money was raised and what the money will be used for. You can also thank any volunteers who assisted with the Book Fair. You might be able to use your newsletter to announce when your next Book Fair is scheduled, or if any other fundraisers are occurring that directly benefit literacy in your school.

Literary programming. Did your library celebrate Read across America Day? Did you acknowledge Children's Book Week? National Poetry Week? African American Read-In Day? National Library Week? If you offered any type of programming or student-centered activities for any kind of reading celebration, use the newsletter to recap your successful programs. Did you have a Mystery Reader? (see chapter 1). Announce the name and title of the distinguished person who was honored to be the coveted Mystery Reader—and provide the number of students caught reading by the Mystery Reader.

Did you have any special guest readers for Breakfast with a Book? Did you have 152 kids participate in a Book Exchange? How many students were inducted into your Readers Hall of Fame? These kinds of things are perfect for an end-of-year newsletter.

Did the kindergartners celebrate the 100th Day of school with 100 books? (see chapter 2). Your kindergarten parents probably knew about the library's 100th Day celebration, but parents of fourth graders might be unaware—tell them in a newsletter!

Did you have an author visit? Even if your author visit happened much earlier in the school year, such an important event is significant enough to detail as a highlight of the literary year.

Other Ideas for Newsletters

Newsletters are a wonderful advocacy tool, a concise way to inform the school community about the many activities of the library, and a simple way to say thank you to the many people who have contributed to the culture of literacy in the library and the school (see Figure 5.8). Certainly you will have written a personal thank-you note to any person or group who has contributed to or volunteered with the library, but a newsletter allows you the opportunity to publicly acknowledge donors, guest readers, and volunteers who shelve books and bake desserts for a Literary Lunch. Not only are you thanking someone, you might also be inspiring other people to participate in the library's programs.

Another Tip for Newsletters

Do *not* include the number of books weeded and discarded. Generally, people like to know that the library is adding new books and items. As with a well-tended garden, you know it's necessary to dutifully weed the collection, but you don't show off your weeds once they are removed. It seems to make people squeamish to think about books being discarded. Stick to announcing new items added.

SCRAPBOOKS AND PHOTO ALBUMS

You are doing amazing things all year in the library, so make sure that you document these events. Digital cameras make it especially easy to snap photographs of students hanging up decorations in the library, huddling together over a book, working on the computer, or wearing a silly hat for Hats Off to Reading Day. Documenting all these activities is the first step, but the next step is even more important: gathering all those photographs together in a photo album or scrapbook that will serve as a reminder of a year's worth of literary activities.

What Is a Library Scrapbook or Photo Album?

While a newsletter is a one- or two-page written document that highlights a year's worth of literary activities, and though a newsletter posted on a Web site might stay posted for many months, it is designed to be a temporary document. A scrapbook or photo album has real lasting power, however. It is a compilation of photographs and other mementoes of the major activities of your library. It can become an advocacy tool and will also be an extremely popular tome with students visiting the library.

How to Plan a Scrapbook or Photo Album

The most important aspect in planning a scrapbook is to take photographs all year long. Keep your digital camera nearby at all times so that

Library End of Year Review

As always, our school library has had a busy, productive year. We are privileged to serve every student from preschool through 6th grade, as well as providing curriculum support to the entire faculty. As we wind down for the summer, we'd like to share some of our statistics as well as highlights.

Statistics:

Number of books circulated: 13,197

Number of NEW books added: 625

Number of Birthday Books added: 81

Most popular books in the library (as determined by the number of times each item was checked out): *Harry Potter and the Sorcerer's Stone*; *Guinness Book of World Records*

We received significant donations from:

Emelio's Pizza

The family of Isabella and Cecelia Simon

Brandon's Books

Wojcik, Shields & Associates

The Mahoney family

Maggie's Bookshop

Our major fundraisers:

Book Fair

Library Spaghetti Dinner

Family Cake Decorating Contest

Literary events:

Annual Family Reading Festival

Monthly Literary Lunches

Pizza party for Reading Hall of Fame students

6th grade Book Club

2nd grade Caldecott Club

Summer Reading: I will enclose a suggested reading list in each student's report card. Of course, we urge you to sign up your child for the public library's summer reading program. Take a book everywhere you go this summer . . . to the beach or the pool or your own backyard. Thanks for all you do to raise a reader!

Happy Reading!

Figure 5.8: Sample library newsletter.

From *Creating a Culture of Literacy: Programming Ideas for Elementary School Librarians* by Anne E. Ruefle. Santa Barbara, CA: Libraries Unlimited. Copyright © 2009.

you can document both the major events (such as an author visit) and the ordinary events (such as a group of first graders trying to find Waldo for the very first time). The genius of digital photography is that you can take hundreds and hundreds of photographs without ever spending a cent on printing. Once you have compiled all your photographs in your digital photo library, you can look through them and print out the very best shots for inclusion in the official library photo album.

Effort should be made to include as many student photos as possible in the album. Most students love to see pictures of themselves. Lots of candid photos of students "caught reading" would be a fun way to include many students (see Figure 5.9). Perhaps you could dedicate a few pages simply to a Reading Roundup and take pictures of students in various places in the library.

Make certain that all significant library events are represented. If you created a Readers Hall of Fame, include small photos of all the inductees. If an author visited the school, document the visit in the album. Did you remember to take pictures during a Reading Drill or a Sidewalk Chalk Fun Day? (see chapter 1). Photographs of all these things should be included.

Figure 5.9: Students reading in the library.

One or two photographs of each Literary Lunch, Book Club meeting, Breakfast with a Book, or Library Lock-In will provide a wonderful panorama of your literary landscape.

Other things to include might be certificates of participation in activities such as a Reading Olympics or a Reading Marathon, any interesting letters received by the library, and newspaper clippings documenting library activities.

How to Implement a Library Scrapbook or Photo Album

Though it takes work to arrange a scrapbook or photo album, you don't need to do it alone. Enlist parent volunteers or your Friends of the Library Club to help put together an annual photo album or scrapbook. The album could be put together over the course of several months or compiled at the end of the school year. If your budget allows, add stickers or other items to the pages. These items, found in scrapbooking and craft stores, will add color and pizzazz to the photo pages. Every picture should have a caption. Create a special shelf in the library for all the library photo albums. Though the scrapbooks and photo albums will be noncirculating, allow students ready access to them and expect to have students pull these books out over and over again. Library photo albums are also great teaching tools. When you explain your library programs to new students or teachers, the photo albums can be a visual explanation of unfamiliar literary events. The library photo albums also provide wonderful documentation for accreditation visits as well as award applications.

Other Ideas for Scrapbooks and Photo Albums

You might not need to ever mount a photo in a physical album. Digital photo frames are growing in popularity as well as capacity. Store the photographs you take on a digital photo frame and display the photo frame in your library or another high-traffic area in the school. New photographs can be added as your literacy events unfold, thus keeping the digital photo display fresh and interesting to your students. If there is an interest, compile the library activity photographs on CDs to distribute at the end of the year as a literary photo album.

If your district or school policies allow for student photographs to be posted on your school's Web site, consider an online photo album in addition to, or instead of, a physical photo album. One advantage of an online photo album is that students and families can access the photos from home and share the literacy activities with a much wider audience.

Another Tip for Scrapbooks and Photo Albums

Much like a newsletter, the photo album or scrapbook serves as a simple advocacy tool, reminding people of the many activities happening in the library. You might consider doing a PowerPoint presentation of your digital library photo album at an opening of the school year meeting or at a curriculum night to introduce your school parents to the upcoming literacy activities you are planning for the school year.

At Meet the Teacher Night, parent-teacher conferences, open houses, grandparent breakfasts, or any other school event that includes parents and other stakeholders, the library photo albums should be on display. Students and parents will pore over these scrapbooks again and again, year after year. As the receptacle of books for the school community, the library should contribute its own special book to the collection—an archive of library programs that documents all the efforts in creating a culture of literacy.

Chapter 6

Involving the Faculty

Build Literary Links between the Library and the Faculty

Collaboration between school librarians and teachers is central to student achievement, and creating a culture of literacy can only occur if the faculty is involved. The possibilities for dynamic collaborations are increased when the faculty is connected to the school library. This chapter provides simple ways to build additional literary links between the school library and the faculty.

60 Second Reviews
Faculty Breakfast with the Books
Faculty Book Club
Faculty Photo Fun

60 SECOND REVIEWS

One of the most frustrating aspects of maintaining an up-to-date library collection is the feeling that many new books and materials are often overlooked, as well as knowing that teachers would benefit from utilizing more material in their classrooms. Offering 60 Second Reviews to your faculty on a regular basis will go a long way toward highlighting these literary gems.

What Is a 60 Second Review?

A 60 second review is a quick and easy way to keep your staff informed about new books coming into the library. Assuming your school has faculty meetings on a regular basis, plan on bringing a new book or 2 or 10 to the meeting to show to the staff in 60 seconds or less.

How to Plan a 60 Second Review

The first thing you should do is discuss with school administrators the feasibility of incorporating a 60 Second Review into every faculty meeting. It is important to emphasize 60 seconds, and it will be equally important to stick to that 60 seconds. No one is happy about a lengthened faculty meeting, and the principal might balk at adding yet another item to the agenda. But 60 seconds is such a reasonable amount of time, it would be difficult to refuse a one-minute addition to a meeting.

If you subscribe to any library journals that review children's literature, such as *The Horn Book, School Library Journal, Teacher-Librarian,* and *BookList,* bring these journals with you to your meeting with the principal. Explain that teachers rarely have time to read these professional journals and that you will continue to do the work of reading reviews and selecting acquisitions, but you would like some time to share new acquisitions with the staff. Continue to stress that you will require only 60 seconds at each meeting.

Once you receive permission to offer a 60 Second Review at each meeting, you need to keep a running list of new books that you feel are important to share with the staff. Keep in mind your audience. If your school is a kindergarten through second grade building, just about any book you share will appeal to every teacher in the school. If your staff is quite large and includes a wide range of teachers, think carefully about selecting books that have broad appeal for multiple grades. You might show books for primary grades one month, and books for intermediate grades the next month.

You can share new books that would be good for an upcoming holiday or season. You might bring a new set of biographies of explorers so that social studies teachers know that such a resource is available. If you know the science teachers in your building are planning a science fair, bring along any new science books that might be of use to them or their students. After the major children's book awards are named each winter, bring along the award-winning titles so anyone not familiar with the titles, or the awards, will know your library has them available to check out. Consider your 60 Second Review a commercial interruption of the very best kind—and market those books to your captive audience!

How to Implement a 60 Second Review

When it comes time for you to share your 60 Second Review, plan the briefest of reviews. You do not need to discuss plot or theme or indexes or organization. Your 60 Second Review should be as simple as possible. You really only need to say the title, what grade level the book is for, and a few quick reasons why you think it might be a worthwhile title for teachers or students. If you are showing just one book, you will be amazed at how much you can say in just one minute. If you are sharing multiple books, all centered on a theme, you can hold up each title in rapid-fire succession and rattle off a few quick details. Before you present for the first time, practice your review with a timer just to give yourself some idea of how much (or how little) can be said in 60 seconds.

Don't worry about sharing the blockbuster books; chances are, most of the faculty will have heard of the extremely popular titles. Your quest is to spotlight titles, both fiction and nonfiction, that are valuable to the curriculum and that might otherwise be missed.

On the day of the faculty meeting, have the book or books prepared and ready to go. After each meeting, display the books in the library for a few days so any interested teacher can have easy access to them.

One benefit of sharing 60 Second Reviews is that your faculty will be reminded that you are attentive to their classroom needs and are an invaluable resource to them. Sharing resources can be the first step in potential collaborative instruction with faculty members.

Other Ideas for a 60 Second Review

It is possible that your school has multiple faculty meetings, or meets by department and you do not attend each meeting. In that case, share your reviews at the meetings you attend and write up a brief flier and share it with the teachers you do not see. If you are able to rotate among meetings, drop by with your stack of books and your 60 Second Review and wow your faculty with a "drive-by review."

Another Tip for a 60 Second Review

If you maintain a library Web site, post your 60 Second Reviews after each meeting so faculty members can be reminded of the titles you shared. Ask teachers and department heads if they have any special areas of interest or upcoming units and share titles to augment their needs. Never pass up an opportunity to connect with the classrooms or the curriculums.

FACULTY BREAKFAST WITH THE BOOKS

So what's the best way to get your faculty into the library? Books? No, that's too obvious. Scheduling a collaborative planning meeting? Hardly. What's a surefire way to bring this significant group of people into the school library? Food and coffee, of course.

What Is a Faculty Breakfast with the Books?

While a schoolwide Breakfast with a Book is a story presentation for the entire school that centers on one book (see chapter 2), and a 60 Second Review can provide brief introductions of one or two books a month, a Faculty Breakfast with the Books is for just the faculty, and it includes a whole lot of books. A Faculty Breakfast with the Books is a time to invite the faculty to the library for an early-morning perusal of a collection of books gathered around a specific theme—and share breakfast at the same time (see Figure 6.1).

How to Plan a Faculty Breakfast with the Books

The main purpose of a Faculty Breakfast with the Books is to share books. You might entice the faculty with food and coffee, but you want them there to look at the books. Carefully consider the rationale for the breakfast gathering. If you are asking a very busy group of people to attend a library function *before* the school day begins, you need to ensure there's a good reason to be there.

A Faculty Breakfast with the Books works best when a need arises in the academic environment in your school. Teachers often ask librarians to pull a collection of books, but a Faculty Breakfast with the Books addresses a larger need—when multiple teachers need to see the materials available in the library. Perhaps your school is developing a schoolwide action plan to improve math scores. You might gather together every single book in your library that has anything remotely to do with mathematics, including non-fiction, picture books, concept books, and biographies of mathematicians, and host a Faculty Breakfast with the Books to let the teachers see the possible titles. Your town might be celebrating the anniversary of an important historical event; gather together every possible resource that touches on the historical era as well as the event itself. The primary teachers have decided to do a month-long study of the oceans; pull together all the books that cover the ocean, ocean animals, ocean habitats, environmental concerns, and picture books with an ocean setting. The number of resources available in your library on a given subject often staggers teachers, but they may not know about those titles until you pull them together.

You are invited to the annual

Faculty Breakfast with the Books
Tuesday morning
October 13

7:00 A.M. - 7:45 A.M.

in the library

Featuring:

math-related books

~ numbers ~ counting ~ concepts ~ geometry

~money ~ sorting ~ time

&

books by Christopher & Jeanette Canyon
(our visiting authors this November)

On the menu:

Bagels from Maria's Deli

Pastries

Fresh fruit

Orange juice & coffee

Figure 6.1: Sample invitation to a Faculty Breakfast with the Books.

From *Creating a Culture of Literacy: Programming Ideas for Elementary School Librarians* by Anne E. Ruefle. Santa Barbara, CA: Libraries Unlimited. Copyright © 2009.

Because it can be very difficult to gather together the entire faculty after school, and lunchtime is often rushed and chaotic, an early-morning gathering might afford you the best opportunity to see as many teachers as possible. Invite the teachers to stop by the library on the scheduled day, and promise a light breakfast they can eat while looking at all the books you will have on display (see Figure 6.2).

Figure 6.2: Teacher browsing at a Faculty Breakfast with the Books.

Keep the breakfast menu simple and the breakfast items easy to carry around while looking at books. Bagels, cinnamon rolls, fresh fruit, or do-nuts or pastries are all fine to offer, as well as juice and coffee. Have baby wipes available for your guests to wipe their hands before looking at books.

Spend several days culling over your collection to gather all the re-sources available on your selected topic. Set up your display the night before the event so that you will not be rushed in the morning. If you have a lot of books, or books that fall into different categories or reading levels, make signs that identify the book groupings so that teachers can easily determine which books they are most interested in viewing. Include any material that might be beneficial for the teachers, including periodicals, DVDs, videos, and software. Print out a list of suitable Web sites that will augment the books.

Send several reminders to teachers about the day and time of the event. The flier you prepare for the faculty should emphasize the theme for the Faculty Breakfast with the Books. Reassure the teachers they only need to drop by and look at the books; they are not committed to spend 45 minutes listening to you lecture about books. Knowing that they are on a tight schedule before school begins will nudge teachers to take a serious look at the books before they need to report to classrooms.

How to Implement a Faculty Breakfast with the Books

Plan the Faculty Breakfast with the Books much like an open house. Don't plan on a formal presentation, but do be available to answer questions and point out books that are of particular interest. During your faculty gathering, keep a running list of any additional titles or subjects that teachers would like you to purchase for the library. Inviting the faculty to play a role in the library's collection development is a form of collaboration that should not be overlooked.

No books should leave the library until the breakfast is over. If a teacher finds a book she wants to check out during the faculty gathering, put a sticky note on the book with the teacher's name and reassure her that the book will be in her mailbox by the end of the day.

Expect one or two teachers to run into the library five minutes before school starts; hand them a cup of coffee and a bagel and tell them to take a quick jog around the display tables. Many folks do not consider themselves morning people and can easily forget an early-morning library event unless reminded more than once. If teachers have a check-in place in your building, hang up a sign on the day of the event that reminds them to stop by the library before classes start.

Don't forget about the Faculty Breakfast with the Books
this morning, 7:00–7:45
Books, coffee, & conversation await you in the library!

Remember to make arrangements to open the library to students slightly later in the morning so you have time to clean up. Any leftover breakfast items can be taken to the faculty lunchroom with a special note of thanks to all of the faculty who stopped by earlier that morning.

Other Ideas for a Faculty Breakfast with the Books

If a breakfast gathering doesn't seem possible for your school, try a faculty gathering during lunchtime. You might have to recruit parents to help cover any lunch or recess duties, but clearing a time in the middle of the day might allow more faculty members a chance to peruse the books on display.

If no immediate idea comes to mind for a theme around which to host a Faculty Breakfast with the Books, you can always host a faculty gathering just to highlight all the new books you've acquired during the school year. Your faculty and administrators will be amazed at the number of new titles you can acquire in the course of a year, and the Faculty Breakfast with the Books becomes a bit of a public relations tool for the library as well as a way to introduce the new books to the staff.

If you have a large number of new faculty members joining the staff, consider hosting an "Introduction to the Library" before the start of the school year so that you have a chance to show off the library and its resources to new staff members. Take time to explain the variety of opportunities and programs available to them. Display any photo albums or scrapbooks from previous years (see chapter 5), and provide a schedule of upcoming literary events. Share with the new teachers the ways in which you interact with the students, suggestions for possible classroom collaborations, and the role that library programming plays in the life of the school.

Another Tip for a Faculty Breakfast with the Books

Consider having a door prize as part of your Faculty Breakfast with the Books. Have faculty members drop their names into a hat as they come to your gathering, and pull out a name or two at the conclusion of the event. You might have a bouquet of flowers, a gift card to a local coffee shop, or a coupon for one free lunch duty. A door prize could be the perfect "dessert" for your gathering.

FACULTY BOOK CLUB

If you can get your students to join one of your Book Clubs (see chapter 3), there's no reason why you can't convince your faculty to join a Book Club of their very own. As the literacy leaders of your school, your faculty should be at the forefront of reading. Because teachers are among the busiest people in the world, it might take some convincing for them to take on one more project, but a school that is trying to create a culture of literacy needs every teacher to be reading, too.

What Is a Faculty Book Club?

A Faculty Book Club is much like any other Book Club: a group of people select a book, read it, and meet to discuss it. The difference between a Faculty Book Club and many other adult Book Clubs is that a Faculty Book Club concentrates on books for children. One advantage of reading books for children is that these novels, even those with complex stories and themes, are typically much easier to read than books written for adults. Even the non-reading faculty members on your staff could be enticed to join knowing that the book selections could be read in a night or two. Best of all, in addition to reading some wonderful stories, teachers will have yet another way to connect with the students they are teaching.

How to Plan a Faculty Book Club

The first thing you should do is make it clear that this is a low-impact Book Club. There are no rules beyond reading a book. No notes need to be taken, no prior questions to consider, no Web quests to follow, no discussion moderators to assign. The point of the Book Club is to read a book and meet to discuss it. Faculty members should be reassured that they might read a book one month, skip a month, and then read the next book on the list.

You can decide on a book for every month and publish the list at the beginning of the school year, or choose a few books at a time to read over several months. You might try an evolving list as the year goes by. You and your faculty will find a rhythm that works for you—the main point is that you are all gathering to read, discuss, and get to know the books that the students are reading.

Your book selections will depend on the circumstances of your school population and the reading level at which your Book Club wishes to read. Allow everyone a voice in the selection process. Educators are especially passionate about the books they love, and no doubt they will make plenty of suggestions. As the librarian, you are probably the one who is most familiar with the wealth and depth of children's literature, and the staff will look to you to help select outstanding titles. Just as with the Book Club for students, you will never, ever run out of choices. Keep in mind that primary teachers can benefit from reading young adult books, and middle grade teachers can get a glimpse into what fourth graders are reading. One of the reasons for a Faculty Book Club is to provide opportunities for teachers to stretch beyond their subject area or grade level and read titles they might not come across in their own classrooms.

If selecting texts proves overwhelming, stick to titles that have already been deemed worthy of major awards. The ALA's Web site maintains lists of all the major book awards for children, including the Newbery Award, Coretta Scott King award winners, and the Printz Award for Young Adult Literature, to name a few. The National Book Award, presented in November of each year, lists its nominees a month in advance of the announcement; the staff might try to read the nominated titles and see if their selection for best book matches that of the National Book Award committee.

A vital aspect of a Faculty Book Club is the meeting to discuss the book (see Figure 6.3). The meeting should be scheduled well in advance so teachers can plan to attend. Let faculty members know that the meeting is open to everyone, even those who haven't finished reading the book. By attending a meeting and listening to a robust discussion, a teacher might walk away determined to get home and finish reading the book.

How to Implement a Faculty Book Club

Once you have arranged a system for selecting titles, concentrate on arranging the actual meetings. Though the library is the most obvious meeting place, your venue doesn't have to be on site. Your staff might be more inclined to meet in a local pub or restaurant, where folks can relax and talk and enjoy the company of other educators. A Friday afternoon meeting might be just the thing for a staff reading get-together. In addition to getting a glimpse into the world of student literature, the participating faculty members will also get to know one another better.

Because you are meeting with adults, you should not need to prepare discussion questions; the conversation will undoubtedly take off by itself. If the discussion meanders far from the book, don't worry. One of the most important by-products of a Faculty Book Club is that you're connecting with the staff and you're connected by a book—that's all that really matters.

Let the school know about the Faculty Book Club. Posting the titles on the school Web site reminds the school community that the teachers are also active learners who continue to develop their own reading habits. You cannot create a culture of literacy without the participation of the main stakeholders; a Faculty Book Club is another way to ensure that every teacher has multiple opportunities to experience reading.

Other Ideas for a Faculty Book Club

If you have a thriving Faculty Book Club as well as a thriving student Book Club, arrange a joint meeting of both groups. Ask the students to select a book that the teachers should read; ask the faculty to prepare a snack to share with the students. If possible, meet after school to give the groups more time to interact and talk about the book. Invite the students to prepare questions to ask the teachers, and ask the students to lead the discussion. The role reversals would be a delightful way for students and teachers to connect with each other through literature.

Another Tip for a Faculty Book Club

If a Faculty Book Club does not seem right for your school, you might try a Faculty Reading Challenge. Set up a reading goal for teachers and

Join the library's
low-impact, low-cost, low-commitment,
high-return, mucho prestigious,
barrels-o-fun

Faculty Book Club!

Our first three titles for the year:

Walk Two Moons by Sharon Creech
meeting date: Friday, September 19

There's a Boy in the Girls' Bathroom by Louis Sachar
meeting date: Friday, October 15

Swear to Howdy by Wendelin Van Draanen
meeting date: Friday, November 17

Copies of each book are available in the school library
as well as in the book room

These first three titles center on the issue of empathy . . .
join us for a relaxing Friday afternoon
of lively discussion and thought-provoking conversation

We've reserved the community room at **Isaac's Place**
from 3:30-5:30 for each meeting date

Hope to see you there!

Have suggestions for future titles? Please let us know!

Figure 6.3: Invitation to a Faculty Book Club.

invite them to reach that goal. Any teacher who reaches the goal would be eligible to enter a drawing for a significant prize such as a gift certificate to a local restaurant or bookstore. You might challenge the teachers to read 25 young adult books in a school year, or read the last 15 years' worth of Newbery Award–winning titles. You could also generate a list of the most popular books in your library and see how many books the teachers can read during the school year. Any number of reading scenarios would work as long as you are challenging the faculty to explore literature with which they might not be familiar.

FACULTY PHOTO FUN

Baseball players have trading cards, movie stars have magazine covers, and college students have Facebook. Your faculty can receive much attention and adulation, as well as help create a culture of literacy, through an annual display called Faculty Photo Fun.

What Is Faculty Photo Fun?

Faculty Photo Fun is an entertaining display of photographs that features each teacher holding a favorite book. The photographs are grouped together and hung in a high-traffic area of the school so that many people have the opportunity to look at the photographs. More than just being a display of faculty photographs, Faculty Photo Fun is a reading challenge for students based on all the books in the faculty photographs.

How to Plan Faculty Photo Fun

The first thing you have to do is establish what time of year the photos will be on display. Though this project can stand alone as a reading-related activity, it also works well when incorporated into a larger reading celebration such as Children's Book Week or National Library Week.

The second, and more difficult, task is to convince your faculty that getting their pictures taken is a good thing. Though many adults balk at having their picture taken, your goal is to take a photograph of each teacher in the school posing with a favorite book. Be persistent! Enlist the help of your administrators to "convince" each teacher that participation is essential. If your staff is small, arrange to take photographs of every single teacher. If your staff is quite large, target certain grade level teachers one year, and then take the other teachers' photographs the following year. Ideally, you should have between 20 and 30 faculty and staff members to photograph each year.

Announce well in advance of the project when you are planning to take the faculty photos. Request that the teachers start to think about what book they would like to feature in their photo. Explain that the books they select *need to appeal to the students in your school.* In other words, though some teachers might be voracious readers of Jane Austen or Kurt Vonnegut, for this project, teachers need to select books with meaning and accessibility for elementary students. (If any teachers announce that they are unfamiliar with current children's literature, suggest they attend the next meeting of your Faculty Book Club!)

Schedule a time to take teacher photographs; it may take a week or so to capture the entire faculty on film. Do not be surprised if you have to remind teachers multiple times about selecting a favorite book, as well as hunt down teachers with your camera in hand. Digital cameras make this project relatively easy and inexpensive. When taking the photographs, make sure that the cover of the book is visible. Before you print a picture, make sure the cover, title, and author are as clear as possible in the photograph. Though each teacher is certainly important, the "star" of the photograph is the book, and you cannot have a glare or distortion of the cover.

Once all the photographs are taken and printed (color printers make this process relatively inexpensive), hang them up. The easiest way to do this is to have a large sheet of colorful banner paper and attach the photos directly to the paper. Label each photograph with the appropriate information: teacher's name, grade or subject area, and the title of the book (in case the photograph is not clear). Number each photograph so that it is clear to the viewer which number goes with which photograph. Once this part is complete, you need to work on the challenge or game that accompanies the faculty photos.

How to Implement Faculty Photo Fun

You've taken your photographs, you've attached them to your display paper, and you've numbered everything. Now you can add the "fun" to the "Faculty Photos." Your task is to write a series of questions for students to answer; the answers to the questions will be contained in the photographs. Begin by looking carefully at each book that is featured. It might help to write a list of all the titles selected by the faculty so that you can make connections among the titles. Compose questions that require the students to look thoughtfully at the photographs to determine the answers. Though most of the questions should be obvious just through careful observation, do not hesitate to write a few questions that require students to visit the library for more information. Suggestions for possible questions include the following:

- Two teachers are holding the same book by Leo Lionni. What's the name of the book?

- Three teachers have selected mysteries. List the three mystery titles.
- One teacher is holding a nonfiction book about dogs. Name the book.
- One teacher is holding a book with a dolphin on the cover. Name the book.
- Two teachers have different books by Patricia Polacco. Name the books.
- One teacher has a book written by Beverly Cleary. Name the book.
- Which three teachers are holding Newbery Award–winning books?
- Two teachers are holding different titles from the same series. Name the series as well as the titles of the two books.
- One teacher is holding the book that won the Caldecott Medal last year. Which teacher is it, and what is the title of the book?

Once you create the questions, type them up and have the challenge sheet available for students to answer. Prepare a box for the completed answer sheets. Give students a week to complete the answer sheet. At the end of the week, award a few small prizes to students who have correctly answered all of the challenge questions. If many students have the same correct answers, put all the winning sheets together and pull out one winner.

Students love this game. You will see clusters of students in front of the faculty photos all week long, finding their teachers, trying to figure out the solutions, and comparing their answers. And though they might not be cognizant of it at the time, what the students are really doing is viewing their teachers as readers. Recognizing teachers as readers helps students understand that literacy is an ongoing process for both children and adults, and a culture of literacy is possible only with the participation of everybody in the school.

Other Ideas for Faculty Photo Fun

If you plan to make this an annual event, vary the way you photograph the teachers each year and display the faculty photos in a themed presentation. Ask each teacher to select a biography one year and display all the photographs under the heading "Great Teachers . . . Great People." Another year, as part of a "Reading is Wild" approach, photograph each teacher outside, posing with a book about a favorite animal. Concentrate on books with food for a "Reading is Delicious" theme. Ask teachers to find a book with food in the title and photograph each teacher in the school's cafeteria.

Try a mystery theme and take a picture of each teacher *hiding* behind a book (see Figure 6.4). The teacher should hold a favorite book as well as a clue to her identity. Students would have to look at both the book and

Figure 6.4: A math teacher hides behind a favorite Newbery book.

the clue to figure out who is hiding behind the book. A fourth grade science teacher who loves dogs could pose with a book, a microscope, and a leash, or a physical education teacher could pose behind a book and hold a whistle and a sneaker.

With any of these approaches you will still want to write a list of questions for the students to answer. If you pursue this activity each year, give your teachers as much advance notification as possible so they can consider their book selection well in advance of the event. Even if teachers are initially reluctant to pose for a photograph, seeing how much fun students have with the pictures will cajole them into being good sports—and will allow you the opportunity to be a literary paparazzi once a year.

Another Tip for Faculty Photo Fun

An added dimension to the guessing-game element of Faculty Photo Fun is to ask for baby pictures to go along with favorite books from a teacher's childhood. Hang up a row of baby pictures and a row of pictures of book covers; ask students to try to match the baby photos to the correct books. You could also put together the same kind of display using copies of teachers' high school senior photographs. Baby pictures are cute, but the high school hairdos are a lot more fun!

Chapter 7

Showcasing Distinguished Authors and Illustrators

Inspire Readers with Programs Designed to Highlight the Very Best Creators of Children's Literature

Author studies are a mainstay of most library and literature curriculums. This chapter outlines a systematic plan to introduce students to the works of different authors and illustrators each month of the school year. This chapter also introduces the Family Reading Festival, which celebrates authors, illustrators, books, and children.

Introducing Authors Program
Family Reading Festival

INTRODUCING AUTHORS PROGRAM

Bringing an author to school for a visit can be a highlight of the year. Preparing for the visit, reading the author's books, making projects based on the stories, hearing the author speak, being able to ask questions, and having books autographed are marvelous aspects of a literary event that will resonate with children for months to come. The reality, though, is that author visits can be expensive, and many schools are unable to make arrangements for a real live author visit. If it proves difficult to bring an author directly into your school, it is possible to introduce your students to the works of authors and illustrators all year long with an Introducing Authors program.

What Is an Introducing Authors Program?

Introducing Authors is a program to develop strong readers by directing students to exceptional authors throughout the course of the school year. Using a variety of methods, including displays, presentations, and book talks, you introduce different authors each month all year long, highlighting their books and using those books as teaching tools for many kinds of lessons and projects.

Why a Schoolwide Introducing Authors Program?

Before implementing an extensive program such as this, you should understand why an Introducing Authors program is beneficial, as well as determine the ways it can be incorporated into the academic life of your school. In many ways, an Introducing Authors program is a perfect way to align your library with many of the standards for the 21st-Century Learners set forth by the American Association of School Librarians. Understanding that reading is the foundation for all education is central to student learning and achievement. Students need to show an appreciation of literature, as well as have opportunities to respond to literature. An ongoing Introducing Authors program can allow for multiple, creative ways for students to make connections among themselves, the world, and their reading ("AASL Standards for the 21st-Century Learner," American Library Association, November 8, 2006. http://www.ala.org/ala/mgrps/divs/aasl/guidelinesandstandards/learningstandards/standards.cfm).

Listed below are reasons to implement an Introducing Authors program.

Introduce Students to Dozens of the Best Authors

There are thousands of children's books published every year in America, but not every book is worthwhile. Helping students develop a critical sense for selecting good books is an important component of creating a culture of literacy. Directing students to books by established authors with a solid reputation for quality stories and illustrations, and encouraging them to read widely, allows students opportunities to grow as readers.

Many adult readers are devoted followers of their favorite author, consuming multiple books by that author and regularly buying each new title as it is published. That kind of passion can be seen in younger readers, too, as they eagerly pursue their favorite author or book series. Without professional guidance, however, many students often flounder in deciding what books to read. By introducing a wide range of authors whose work represents different backgrounds and includes a variety of genres, you provide students the freedom to choose from within a large framework of distinguished authors.

Continuous Thread of Literacy through the Grades

Strong language arts programs and reading teachers often immerse their students in classrooms rich in literature and language. But those teachers typically have their students for one year before the students move to another grade and another set of teachers. School librarians, on the other hand, often have the opportunity to work with students for many years, watching them grow and develop as readers and learners. Introducing each grade to a variety of authors every year will ensure that your students have a continual thread of literacy as they progress through your school. Students will learn to make connections with literature, authors, illustrators, and genres from one grade to the next. As students progress through your school, learning about authors and books at each grade level, they will also recognize the importance of connecting current reading to previous reading. They might also look forward to the more advanced reading they will experience in years to come.

Provide a Variety of Opportunities for Students to Respond to Literature and Interact with Other Readers

For students to develop as readers, they need opportunities to respond to what they read. Those responses can be simple, such as a conversation with classmates about a favorite book while waiting for the bus. The responses can also be as elaborate as a six-week research project culminating in a multimedia presentation on weather as depicted in the nonfiction books of Seymour Simon. Using the Author program as a focus, you can provide students multiple opportunities to respond to literature in a variety of ways. There are countless formats for student responses. You might host a Literary Lunch based on an author's books (see chapter 3) or select a story from a popular author for a Breakfast with a Book event (see chapter 2). Students can write book reports, create podcasts reviewing favorite books, paint pictures in the style of an illustrator, or visit an author's Web site to read an interview with the author and search forthcoming titles.

Possibilities for Collaboration between the Librarian and Classroom Teachers

Using the authors and their books as a basis, the opportunities for effective collaborative teaching between teachers and the librarian are enormous. Thoughtful collaboration might include multiple teachers and involve several subject areas. Certainly it takes concentrated effort to collaborate with multiple teachers, but the impact on student learning is profound.

The librarian might introduce the books of Ezra Jack Keats to second grade students, for instance, explaining Keats' collage techniques and giving interesting details about his early life. The art teacher could have the second graders create pictures based on those collage techniques. A reading teacher could ask the same second graders to write an invitation to a hypothetical birthday party, much like Peter in *A Letter to Amy*. A second grade social studies lesson might be able to point to *Whistle for Willie,* another Keats book, to describe a city setting.

How to Plan an Introducing Authors Program

Hundreds of authors are worthy of study, but during the course of one school year you can do justice to only a limited number of authors. Develop criteria for selecting the authors you want to highlight during the year. You will need to have some framework for deciding which authors to include in your program. The following sections detail criteria to consider when choosing authors.

Individual Authors with a Significant Body of Work

If you intend for students to be excited about the author's books, you need to make sure there are enough books to meet the demand. A highlighted author should have a minimum of 8–10 published books. Many established authors, such as Avi and Jane Yolen, have more than 100 books each to their credit, as do illustrators such as Jerry Pinkney and Tomie dePaola. Introducing authors with such a wealth of titles provides multiple instructional opportunities as well as ensuring that virtually every interested child will find some book with which to connect. Authors with a significantly smaller number of published books can also be included in the program, with the understanding that there might be waiting lists for very popular books.

Authors Who Will Provide a Variety of Genres for Students

Authors write nonfiction, realistic fiction, historical, humor, adventure, fantasy, mystery, and science fiction. Illustrators might use any mixture of watercolor, photography, anime, collage, paper pop-ups, or pen and ink. During the course of a school year, make sure you bring to the forefront authors whose work will collectively introduce a variety of genres. If one author writes exclusively science fiction, the next month introduce a mystery writer. Not knowing which books will appeal to each reader means introducing many different genres so that every student might find something appealing. Even better, you might be able to entice your readers to sample a new selection.

Authors Who Will Appeal to a Variety of Reading Levels

Your students will have different reading levels—some advanced, some struggling, some reading exactly at grade level. As you determine which authors you want to introduce, make a conscious effort to select authors who will appeal to the many kinds of students you serve. If you promote a particularly challenging author one month who appeals to advanced readers, then the next month, highlight an author who appeals to reluctant readers. You will serve many different kinds of learners, and there will be authors who will appeal to each of them.

Authors Who Represent Diverse Backgrounds

More than likely, your students will represent a variety of backgrounds, and your authors should reflect that diversity. If your students are homogeneous, it might be even more important to present diverse authors. Consider introducing authors who can provide glimpses into diverse worlds and situations through literature, such as Appalachia (Cynthia Rylant), Asian American life (Laurence Yep), urban life (Walter Dean Myers), single-parent households (Patricia Polacco), or Native American life (Joseph Bruchac). Be attentive to gender, as well. If you introduce only male illustrators to second graders, or only female writers to fifth graders, your students might have a distorted view of who creates illustrations and literature. Considering there are so many accomplished authors, you should have no trouble finding representation from a variety of groups.

Individual Authors Whose Work You Like

Educators are obligated to be objective in their teaching, and selecting authors to introduce to children is no exception. When faced with selecting a limited number of authors to study from a list that includes dozens and dozens of authors for potential study, you might need to rely on the tried-but-true "gut reaction" to help you narrow your decisions. As long as your authors collectively represent different genres, reading levels, and backgrounds, use your best instincts to make your decisions. If you love the work of a particular illustrator or author and you are certain that your first grade students will be delighted with her books, then by all means include her in your list. Your passion for books will be conveyed most clearly when you are introducing authors whose work you especially admire.

After you compile a list of authors to introduce to your students, it is time to work with teachers to establish the best method for embedding this program into the school curriculum.

How to Implement an Introducing Authors Program

As you begin a comprehensive authors program, you will need to determine the best ways in which to introduce authors to your students. Below are some questions to consider.

How Often Will You Introduce Authors?

You might try introducing a new author every month, or perhaps consider introducing two or three authors each semester to allow for an in-depth exploration of each author. If you are working in tandem with classroom teachers, follow their lead and be prepared to help introduce new authors whenever it works best into their schedule.

To Which Classes Will You Introduce Authors?

Will you be able to introduce a new author every month to every grade, or will you concentrate on just one or two grades? Consider the instructional opportunities for introducing authors. If the third grade teachers are eager to include author studies in their language arts classes, then by all means focus your attention on the third grade. Work with the teachers to select the authors to introduce during a school year, and set up a schedule for the author presentations. Consider the ways in which the literacy of your students is strengthened if every third grader in your school becomes familiar with the same authors. Students would share similar reading experiences and be familiar with the same authors, the same series, and the same books. The opportunity for literature extensions and projects and responses grows exponentially.

You might begin a formal Introducing Authors program by simply concentrating on one grade, but over the course of a few years, add more classrooms or grades to your program. Taking time to develop your author program will also allow you the opportunity to develop your collection so that you have a suitable number of books for each author you introduce.

What Format Will You Use to Introduce the Authors You Include in Your Program?

You might set aside the first week of each month to introduce a different author to each class during a regularly scheduled visit to the library. As students visit the library, take time to talk about the author or illustrator and share a story or two from the author. Show each class where the author's books are in the collection, or, if possible, have a reserve section where you might house the author's books for a month. If you have a bulletin board or display area, create a display about the author. Use newspaper clippings, biography sheets provided by the publisher or the author's Web site, copies of book covers, bookmarks, or anything else related to the author. Creating a new monthly display would be a good ongoing assignment for parent volunteers or your Friends of the Library Club.

If you have a flexible schedule, you might arrange to visit classrooms and do a special author presentation once a month. Imagine how students will perceive the importance of the author presentation if you visit them in *their* classroom; that special emphasis will create added excitement to the presentation. Bring along a large crate of the author's books when you visit the classroom. Spend 30 minutes telling stories about the author, reading a book or two, and pointing out interesting aspects of a particular book. Ask the teacher to create a shelf or special area to hold a set of the author's books for classroom use for the month. Be on the lookout for posters of the author's books to be loaned to a classroom for that month. Bring along any handouts you have, as well as any DVDs, audiotapes, or videos that relate to the author or illustrator.

During subsequent classes in your library, direct the students to an author's Web site. Invite students to draw pictures of their favorite book each month (see Figure 7.1). Work with the art teachers to include art projects based on the artwork of a particular illustrator.

Figure 7.1: Students create pictures based on Eric Carle's illustrations.

If your school is quite large and it proves impossible to offer individual presentations to each class or grade, concentrate on developing extensive displays in your library devoted to authors, and designate a specific area of your space for a rotating collection of different authors' books. When you are overwhelmed by multiple students needing your help in several areas of the library, and one student says, "Do you have any good books?" you can quickly point to your highlighted author section and say, "Start there. You'll be sure to find something good on that shelf." With the right amount of marketing and book talking, students will come to rely on this author section as the first place to look for a good book.

Other Ideas for Author Programs

List your authors on your Web site. Set up links from your library Web site to favorite author Web sites. Use your newsletter to inform your school families of authors currently under study, and invite students and parents to visit your Web site for an easy link to authors' Web sites. Encourage families to check out books from the public library so they can share the same books at home that the students are studying at school.

Children's authors are remarkably accessible through literature and library conferences, bookstore signings, and special appearances at public library events. When you attend these kinds of events, pick up the free information packets that most authors provide regarding themselves and their books. Publishers often provide author profiles to promote a new book. Keep all of these items in a large three-ring binder as an easy reference source for author information, available to both students and teachers.

Another Tip for Introducing Authors Programs

When a beloved book you often use with children is beyond repair and ready to be discarded, consider dismantling the book and laminating any pages that are still in good shape. Lend a few of these pages at a time to classroom teachers who are studying that book or author. If students are working on a writing or art project based on that book, these individual laminated pages might be used as an instructional tool or sample illustration.

See suggested author and illustrator lists at the end of this chapter.

FAMILY READING FESTIVAL

Imagine your school on a late spring evening, filled with teachers, administrators, students, siblings, and parents. All around you, families are picking up books, listening to a story, helping to paint a mural, watching a puppet show, reading students' stories hanging on the walls, or making an art project based on a book. The entire evening is a celebration of reading.

A Family Reading Festival can be a culmination of a school year's worth of literacy activities.

What Is a Family Reading Festival?

A Family Reading Festival is a literary showcase for your school. It is typically an evening event that offers literacy activities for parents and children. Though there are many ways to host a Reading Festival, at the center of the festival are children and books. No matter which format you consider, envision multiple ways in which to include your school families. Connecting with families is a vital component of creating a culture of literacy.

How to Plan a Family Reading Festival

Hosting a successful Family Reading Festival means planning, collaboration, imagination, and organization—the kinds of things you do on daily basis. For a successful Family Reading Festival, you will just need to do these things on a larger scale. You will need to involve other members of your faculty to help with planning and arrangements, but having an event that fosters and supports literacy is certain to receive support from both administrators and faculty.

There are multiple things to consider as you plan for your school's Family Reading Festival.

What is your target audience, and how many people can you accommodate? Do you want to have a Reading Festival that includes the entire school? Perhaps you will invite kindergarten through third grade students. Or do you want to focus on just second graders and their families? Your decision will have to factor in such things as the space available to you, your student population, and how many adults you have to help you oversee the evening's activities. Once you decide how many people you can handle and what age groups you will target, you will have an easier time deciding the more complex questions, such as what activities to include. Remember that you are not just considering the number of second graders in your school; you are planning for second graders *and their parents*, as well as siblings and interested grandparents. Consider the number of people who might attend and plan accordingly.

Where will you hold your event? Your administrators will be helpful in determining the best ways to use your school facilities. Do you want to contain all the activities in a large multipurpose room or gymnasium?

Do you want families to rotate through classrooms and the library? Can you hold any part of the event outside? Consider such things as access to parking for parents and the easiest way for families to enter and leave your school building. Where you host your event will play a major role in determining which literacy activities to plan.

When will you hold your event? You can schedule your Family Reading Festival for any time of the school year. If you plan it for the beginning of the school year, it can serve as a kickoff to the many literacy events you envision for the rest of the year. If you schedule it for the middle of the school year, it can be a way to energize your faculty and families during the winter months. If you plan it for the end of the year, it can serve as the culminating literacy activity of the school year, highlighting all of the wonderful reading activities your students have worked on for months. You might even be ambitious enough to plan more than one Family Reading Festival a year, depending on the response from your school families. Whenever you decide to schedule your event, make sure you publicize it so your school families are sure to attend (see Figure 7.2).

How long should your event last? Plan for an evening that lasts anywhere from ninety minutes to two hours. Consider the ages of the students you invite—you don't want to schedule an evening that lasts until 9:00 P.M. if you plan to involve kindergartners. A time frame such as 6:00–8:00 P.M. will suit most families.

Who will help with the event? You will certainly need a planning committee to help make arrangements for such a large-scale event. You will need folks to handle big details such as publicity and basic tasks such as gathering enough scissors or glue for any art projects you envision. You will also need to involve other adults to help oversee activities throughout the night. Though many schools have dedicated parents who willingly volunteer for school projects, consider asking your faculty to play a large role in running the Reading Festival events. One reason to rely on faculty rather than parents is that you want to ensure that parents are free to participate with their children during the Festival. Another, more important reason to ask the faculty to volunteer to work the Festival is that you want to make a clear statement to your school families that the entire faculty is committed to creating a culture of literacy. Invite every faculty and staff member to participate at the Festival. Include the physical education teacher, the school nurse, the math teachers, and the guidance counselor. Making connections with the larger school staff can go a long way in building community, as well as strengthening the visibility of the school's literacy programs.

You are invited to our 5th annual

Family Reading Festival

Friday

6:00 P.M. - 8:00 P.M.

Join us for an evening of reading-related games,

art projects, and activities

all based on authors, illustrators, and books.

~ Listen to a story by our principal, Ms. Penny ~
~ Make a bookmark with shaving cream and paint ~
~ Learn how to make your own homemade paper ~
~ Try a *Very Hungry Caterpillar* relay race ~
~ Use pasta to make a Tomie DePaola picture ~
~ Enjoy a story presentation brought to you by
Mr. Amicon's first graders ~
~ Stop by the Book Fair in the library ~
~ Enter a drawing for new books ~
~ Add a page to our Reading Festival book ~
and much more!

Figure 7.2: Sample invitation to a Family Reading Festival.

From *Creating a Culture of Literacy: Programming Ideas for Elementary School Librarians* by Anne E. Ruefle. Santa Barbara, CA: Libraries Unlimited. Copyright © 2009.

What kinds of activities should you include? Developing the reading-related activities for the evening is the crucial aspect of any Family Reading Festival. If you want to build literacy connections between parents and children, and between the families and the school, the activities need to be accessible, fun, and worthwhile. Consider using your author and illustrator studies as a basis to develop the activities for the Family Reading Festival. The advantage of developing your activities around the authors you have introduced during the school year is that your students will already be familiar with those authors and their books, which will intensify their interest in the activities.

How to Implement a Family Reading Festival

A Family Reading Festival can operate much like a literary showcase for the school. In addition to the many reading-related activities that are available for students and families, teachers should be encouraged to display student work related to literacy. Remind teachers months in advance to save any work they might like to display at the Family Reading Festival. Written book reports, dioramas, posters, class books, and collaborative art and reading projects can be part of the background for the festival. Of course, all of the library's scrapbooks or photo albums must be on display for families to see (see chapter 5).

There are many possible formats for a Family Reading Festival. You might have a guest speaker who will address the entire group as the kickoff to the evening. You might have scheduled activities, where students and families rotate through individual classrooms that offer a story and reading activity every 30 minutes. Your curriculum director might hold information sessions in the school library every 20 minutes for interested parents. Your committee might plan multiple activities that occur simultaneously, much like a carnival or festival, where students and parents are free to roam around, visiting the various booths or tables or classrooms that offer activities based on the authors and books you have introduced during the school year. There are countless scenarios for a Family Reading Festival, *and every single format is acceptable.* The important thing is that you are attempting to gather together your school community to celebrate books and children and literacy.

Ideas for Family Reading Festival Activities

The crucial aspects of the Festival are the activities. Below you will find a sampling of activities that should spark ideas for a Family Reading

Festival that you can develop for your school. Envision your school's gymnasium or multipurpose room. The room has large tables arranged around the perimeter. Each table holds a collection of books and various art supplies, including construction paper, glue sticks, scissors, crayons, and even cold spaghetti! The room is full of children and parents moving from table to table, looking through books and making simple art projects based on the books. A different faculty member works at each table, facilitating the activity, offering gentle help, and answering any questions about the activities in the room. The atmosphere in the room is much like that of a traditional carnival or festival: good humor and excitement as students decide which activity to select first.

At a booth celebrating the books of Tomie dePaola, for instance, students may grab a handful of cooked and cooled plain spaghetti and stick it to a piece of construction paper in a tribute to the pasta in *Strega Nona*. (Cooked pasta will stick to paper just as if it has been glued.) Have on display all of the *Strega Nona* books, as well as any other Tomie dePaola titles in your library. After students make their pasta art, they may take it with them or add it to a Tomie dePaola art wall you create at the Festival.

At the next booth, honoring author and illustrator Lois Ehlert, students might find bright sheets of neon colored paper. Students will also find a collection of Lois Ehlert books on display, including *Planting a Rainbow* and *Growing Vegetable Soup*. Using scissors, the neon colored paper, and stencils cut from tag board, students make a flower garden or vegetable garden artwork based on these colorful books.

At a third booth, students might find a large bus made out of cardboard. A large "NO" is printed on one side of the bus, and on the other side is a large "YES." For this activity, students are first asked to draw a picture of Mo Willems's beloved Pigeon character. Visit Mo Willems's Web site for easy directions to draw Pigeon. After the children make their Pigeon, they are asked to write a sentence or two deciding whether Pigeon should be able to drive the bus. Students place their Pigeon drawings on the side of the cardboard bus that corresponds with "yes" or "no," and at the end of the evening you announce whether Pigeon "received" permission from your students to drive the bus. Of course, the booth also has on display a collection of all Mo Willems's books for children and parents to peruse.

Down the hallway there might be several classrooms with a different story and reading activity happening in each one. A math teacher might select a book such as *Freight Train,* by Donald Crews. After reading the book to the assembled students and parents, he invites each student to examine how shapes play a role in the artwork of the train. With scissors and construction paper, students and parents cut out rectangles and circles to create a train much like the freight train that travels though this Caldecott Honor book. The teamwork of the child and the adult is the most important part of these kinds of activities.

Your principal might select *Henry and Mudge* to highlight the books of Cynthia Rylant. Using a second grade classroom as her space, she has many of the *Henry and Mudge* titles and a Mudge doll on display, as well as lots of nonfiction books about pets. After the principal reads *Henry and Mudge* to her audience, she asks the children to talk about their own pets. If some students don't have a pet, she can ask them what kind of pet they might like to have. She passes out paper and crayons and asks the children to draw a picture of their favorite pet. She can ask them to write a brief description of their pet that can be compiled into a Family Reading Festival book at the conclusion of the evening.

One room might simply be full of books and blankets and pillows where a parent and child might grab a book, plop to the floor, and read for a few minutes.

Families might wander to the cafeteria to listen to a reading of *If You Give a Mouse a Cookie,* written by Laura Numeroff. On tables around the cafeteria, have plain sugar cookies and bowls of icing and sprinkles and invite families to decorate cookies of their own.

On the front lawn of the school, parents and children can team up for a silly relay race based on *The Very Hungry Caterpillar,* by Eric Carle. Teachers or volunteers hold up a series of hula hoops, representing the food the caterpillar eats, for participants to crawl through. Both children *and* parents must take turns crawling through the hula hoops. There are no prizes for this relay race, just lots of laughter as everyone enjoys a fun twist to this children's classic.

After the Eric Carle relay race, families can visit the art room, where the art teacher is demonstrating how to make homemade paper, much like Denise Fleming creates for her books such as *Lunch* and *Small, Small Pond.* Of course, displayed around the art room are all of Denise Fleming's books, as well as several coloring sheets printed out from her Web site.

The evening whirls by as every family moves around the building, taking turns reading and creating, sharing, enjoying, and celebrating the culture of literacy that is evident in your school.

Other Ideas for a Family Reading Festival

Ask your parent-teacher association to donate several new books to use as door prizes for the evening. Every family that comes to the Festival enters their name in the drawing. Give out book prizes throughout the night or at the conclusion of the Festival.

Consider creating a program schedule to hand out to families as they arrive for your Family Reading Festival. List all the activities as well as the rooms in which the activities are located. If there is a scheduled event, such as a guest speaker or a student performance, list the time and location. An official program will also give you a good place to thank anyone who has helped contribute to the Family Reading Festival.

If students will be making lots of art projects throughout the night, distribute bags they can use to keep track of their projects—both the parents and the cleanup crew will thank you!

Keep your camera on hand throughout the night. Photographs of children working with their parents will make some of the most meaningful photographs you take all year.

Another Tip for a Family Reading Festival

A Book Fair could be part of the evening's events if you have enough volunteers. The Book Fair should *not* be the focus of the Festival, but it could be just one of the many places a family might visit during the evening. In fact, the profits from a one-night Book Fair might generate the funds to pay for the supplies used at the Festival.

Finally, consider working with the school's music teacher to have a simple sing-along to conclude the evening, or a brief song production to present to the parents. There are many books that include songs and singing, and a brief presentation would be the perfect way to end your Family Reading Festival.

Perhaps the most extraordinary part of a Family Reading Festival is the opportunity for the *students* to lead the *parents* through the activities. Because each reading activity is based on an author or book that has already been presented to students during the course of the school year, the students are already familiar with the subject matter. Over and over again you will see excited students grab a parent's hand and say, "I want to make a Leo Lionni painting" or "I love *Lilly's Purple Plastic Purse-*. Let's go to the *Lilly* reading room." Though parents are essential in the development of readers, the children themselves can play a magnificent role in creating and sustaining a culture of literacy when they have the right direction and support (see Figures 7.3–7.6).

Figure 7.3: Student painting at a Family Reading Festival.

Figure 7.4: Student at the Mo Willems booth at a Family Reading Festival.

Figure 7.5: Mother working with daughters on a project.

Figure 7.6: Families working together at a Family Reading Festival.

Suggestions for Authors

The following list is not comprehensive, but it is a good place to get started.

Authors and Illustrators for Kindergarten, First Grade, and Second Grade Students

Aliki
Jan Brett
Marc Brown
Eric Carle
Bryan Collier
Donald Crews
Nina Crews
Tomie dePaola
Lois Ehlert
Ian Falconer
Denise Fleming
Don Freeman
Mem Fox
Paul Galdone
Gail Gibbons
Kevin Henkes
Tana Hoban
Pat Hutchins
Trina Schart
   Hyman
Ann Jonas

Steve Jenkins
Ezra Jack Keats
Steven Kellogg
Betsy and Ted
   Lewin
E. B. Lewis
Leo Lionni
Anita Lobel
Arnold Lobel
Loren Long
James Marshall
Bill Martin, Jr.
Bruce McMillan
Robert Munsch
Kevin O'Malley
Laura Numeroff
Margie Palatini
Dav Pilkey
Andrea Davis
   Pinkney
Brian Pinkney

Gloria Pinkney
Jerry Pinkney
Chris Raschka
Faith Ringold
Cynthia Rylant
Maurice Sendak
David Shannon
David Small
Lane Smith
Janet Stevens
Nancy Tafuri
David Wiesner
Mo Willems
Vera B. Williams
Don and Audrey
   Wood
Chris Van
   Allsburg
Ed Young
Paul O. Zelinsky

Authors for Third Grade, Fourth Grade, and Fifth Grade Students

David Adler
Susan Adler
Clyde Robert
   Bulla
Betsy Byars
Ann Cameron
Christopher
   and Jeanette
   Canyon
Matt Christopher

Beverly Cleary
Andrew Clements
Bruce Coville
Paula Danziger
Roald Dahl
Cynthia DeFelice
Kate DiCamillo
Jean Craighead
   George
Patricia Reilly Giff

Paul Goble
Dan Greenburg
Dan Gutman
Karen Hess
Jennifer L. Holm
James Howe
Johanna Hurwitz
E. L. Konigsburg
Gail Carson
   Levine

Lois Lowry
Anne Mazer
Megan McDonald
Patricia
    McKissack
Madeleine L'Engle
Marissa Moss
Katherine
    Paterson

Connie Porter
Jack Prelutsky
J. K. Rowling
Ron Roy
Louis Sachar
Jon Scieszka
Janet Shaw
Seymour Simon
Valerie Tripp

Gertrude Chan-
    dler Warner
Laura Ingalls
    Wilder
Betty Ren Wright
Jane Yolen

Authors for Sixth Grade and Older Students

Lloyd Alexander
Laurie Halse
    Anderson
Avi
John Bellairs
Caroline Cooney
Robert Cormier
Sharon Creech
Christopher Paul
    Curtis
Karen Cushman
Sarah Dessen
Sharon Draper
Lois Duncan
Nancy Farmer
Sharon Flake
John Green
Nikki Grimes

Margaret Peterson
    Haddix
Mary Downing
    Hahn
Anthony Horowitz
Will Hobbs
Brian Jacques
Angela Johnson
Gordon Korman
Mike Lupica
Stephenie Meyer
Walter Dean
    Myers
Phyllis Reynolds
    Naylor
Joan Lowry Nixon
Scott O'Dell
Gary Paulsen

Richard Peck
Tamora Pierce
Pam Munoz Ryan
William Sleator
Zilpha Keatley
    Snyder
Gary Soto
Jerry Spinelli
Mildred Taylor
Cynthia Voight
Wendelin Van
    Draanen
Jacqueline
    Woodson
Vivian Vande
    Velde
Laurence Yep
Paul Zindel

Bibliography

Anderson, Laurie Halse. *Thank You, Sarah: The Woman Who Saved Thanksgiving.* New York: Simon & Schuster, 2002.

Brown, Don. *One Giant Leap: The Story of Neil Armstrong.* New York: Houghton Mifflin, 1998.

Bulla, Clyde Robert. *The Sword in the Tree.* New York: HarperCollins, 1956.

Carle, Eric. *The Very Hungry Caterpillar.* New York: Philomel, 1967.

Cleary, Beverly. *Beezus and Ramona.* New York: Morrow Junior Books, 1955. (And other Ramona titles in this series.)

Cooper, Susan. *The Dark Is Rising.* New York: Margaret K. McElderry Books, 1973.

Crews, Donald. *Freight Train.* New York: Greenwillow Books, 1978.

Cushman, Karen. *Catherine, Called Birdy.* New York: Clarion Books, 1994.

Cushman, Karen. *The Midwife's Apprentice.* New York: Clarion Books, 1995.

De Angeli, Marguerite. *The Door in the Wall.* New York: Doubleday, 1949.

dePaola, Tomie. *Strega Nona.* Englewood Cliffs, NJ: Prentice-Hall, 1975.

DiCamillo, Kate. *The Tale of Despereaux.* Cambridge: Candlewick Press, 2003.

DiTerlizzi, Tony, and Holly Black. *The Field Guide.* New York: Simon & Schuster, 2003. (And other Spiderwick titles from this series.)

DuPrau, Jeanne. *The City of Ember.* New York: Random House, 2003.

Ehlert, Lois. *Growing Vegetable Soup.* New York: Harcourt, 1987.

Ehlert, Lois. *Planting a Rainbow.* New York: Harcourt, 1988.

Fleming, Denise. *Lunch.* New York: Henry Holt and Company, 1992.

Fleming, Denise. *Small, Small Pond.* New York: Henry Holt and Company, 1993.

Funke, Cornelia. *Inkheart.* New York: Scholastic, 2003.

Galdone, Paul. *The Three Bears.* New York: Clarion Books, 1972.

Haddix, Margaret Peterson. *Among the Hidden.* New York: Simon & Schuster, 1988.

Hanford, Martin. *Where's Waldo Now?* Cambridge: Candlewick Press, 1987.

Henkes, Kevin. *Lilly's Purple Plastic Purse*. New York: Greenwillow, 1996.

Horowitz, Anthony. *Stormbreaker*. New York: Philomel Books, 2000.

Hunter, Erin. *Into the Wild*. New York: HarperCollins, 2003. (And other Warriors titles from this series.)

Jacques, Brian. *Redwall*. New York: Philomel Books, 1986. (And other Redwall titles in this series.)

Jenkins, Steve, and Robin Page. *What Do You Do with a Tail Like This?* Boston: Houghton Mifflin, 2003.

Keats, Ezra Jack. *A Letter to Amy*. New York: Viking Press, 1964.

Keats, Ezra Jack. *Whistle for Willie*. New York: Harcourt, 1968.

Keene, Carolyn. *The Secret of the Old Clock*. New York: Grossett & Dunlap, 1930. (And other Nancy Drew titles in this series.)

Kinney, Jeff. *Diary of a Wimpy Kid: Greg Heffles Journal*. New York: Amulet Books, 2007.

Krull, Kathleen. *Wilma Unlimited: How Wilma Rudolph Became the World's Fastest Woman*. New York: Harcourt Brace & Company, 1996.

Lasky, Kathryn. *Dreams in the Golden Country: The Diary of Zipporah Feldman, A Jewish Immigrant Girl*. New York: Scholastic, 1998. (And other Dear America titles in this series.)

Lewis, C. S. *The Lion, the Witch and the Wardrobe*. New York: Macmillan, 1950.

Meyer, Stephenie. *Twilight*. New York: Little, Brown and Company, 2005.

Mosel, Arlene. *Tikki Tikki Tembo*. New York: Henry Holt, 1968.

Naylor, Phyllis Reynolds. *The Boys Start the War*. New York: Bantam Doubleday Dell, 1993. (And other Boys Against Girls titles in this series.)

Numeroff, Laura Joffe. *If You Give a Mouse a Cookie*. New York: HarperCollins, 1985.

Park, Barbara. *Junie B. Jones and the Stupid Smelly Bus*. New York: Random House, 1992. (And other Junie B. Jones titles in this series.)

Paulsen, Gary. *Hatchet*. New York: Atheneum Books, 1987.

Pilkey, Dav. *The Adventures of Captain Underpants*. New York: Blue Sky Press, 1997.

Rowling, J. K. *Harry Potter and the Deathly Hallows*. New York: Arthur A. Levine Books, 2007. (And other Harry Potter titles in this series.)

Rylant, Cynthia. *Henry and Mudge: The First Book of Their Adventures*. New York: Simon & Schuster, 1987.

Sachar, Louis. *Holes*. New York: Farrar, Straus and Giroux, 1998.

Scieszka, Jon. *Math Curse*. New York: Viking, 1995.

Scieszka, Jon. *The Not-So-Jolly Roger*. New York: Viking, 1991. (And other Time Warp Trio titles in this series.)

Scieszka, Jon. *The True Story of the Three Little Pigs*. New York: Viking, 1989.

Sendak, Maurice. *Where the Wild Things Are*. New York: HarperCollins, 1963.

Seuss, Dr. *The Cat in the Hat*. Boston: Houghton Mifflin, 1957.

Shannon, David. *No, David*. New York: Blue Sky Press, 1998.

Shaw, Janet. *Meet Kirsten: An American Girl*. Middleton, WI: Pleasant Company, 1986. (And other American Girl titles in this series.)

Snicket, Lemony. *The Bad Beginning*. New York: HarperCollins, 1999. (And other Series of Unfortunate Events titles in this series.)

Sobol, Donald. *Encyclopedia Brown Solves Them All*. New York: Dutton, 1968. (And other Encyclopedia Brown titles in this series.)

Warner, Gertrude Chandler. *The Boxcar Children*. Morton Grove, IL: Albert Whitman and Company, 1942. (And other Boxcar Children titles in this series.)

White, E. B. *Charlotte's Web*. New York: HarperCollins, 1952.

Wilder, Laura Ingalls. *Little House on the Prairie*. New York: HarperCollins, 1935. (And other Little House titles in this series.)

Wright, Betty Ren. *The Dollhouse Murders*. New York: Holiday House, 1983.

Index

About the Author

ANNE E. RUEFLE has been a teacher-librarian for more than 20 years and is a frequent presenter at library conferences and workshops. In 1999, the Ohio State University's Department of Education awarded her the Mary Karrer Award, presented to the teacher or librarian in the state of Ohio who best inspires children to read. In 2008, the National Catholic Educational Association named her a National Distinguished Teacher of the Year.